Zen and the Bible

Zen and the Bible

A priest's experience

J. K. Kadowaki s.j.

Translated from the Japanese by

Joan Rieck

Routledge & Kegan Paul

London, Boston and Henley

First published in Japanese in 1977 by Shunjūsha, Tokyo,
as Koan to Seisho no Shindoku (*'Body-Reading Koans*
and the Bible — A Christian's Experience with Zen').

This English translation first published in 1980
by Routledge & Kegan Paul Ltd, 39 Store Street, London WC1E 7DD,
Broadway House, Newtown Road, Henley-on-Thames, Oxon RG9 1EN and
9 Park Street, Boston, Mass. 02108, USA

Set in IBM Journal by Columns
Printed in the United States of America by
Vail-Ballou Press.

British Library Cataloguing in Publication Data

Kadowaki, J K

Zen and the Bible.
1. Rinzai (Sect)
2. Zen Buddhism — Relations — Christianity
3. Christianity and other religions — Zen
Buddhism 4. Koan 5. Bible — Criticism,
interpretation, etc.
I. Title
294.3'927   BQ9369.4.C5   79-40874

ISBN 0 7100 0402 8

Contents

Preface

A number of years ago, I went to West Germany to do research on Meister Eckhart, a German mystic of the Middle Ages. While there I was invited by the Catholic theologian, Professor J. Ratzinger (now a cardinal), to lecture on 'Zen and Christianity' to a group of his doctoral students. In that talk, I explained Zen by contrasting it with the thought of Thomas Aquinas and, in spite of my poor German, professor and students alike listened with great interest. The seminar at which I spoke was held annually at the end of the school term. We all stayed together at a hotel overnight, spending many hours in discussion. Towards the end of the seminar, Professor Ratzinger said, 'How interesting it would be if we could compare the ideas of Zen with those of the Bible. If that could be done, it would be a great event, not only for the dialogue between Zen and Christianity, but also in respect to the ideological exchange between East and West.' This comment struck me deeply although then I had not the slightest idea of how Christian Scripture and Zen thought might resemble each other. Later, it completely left my mind and I did not think about it for a long time.

Zen koans are *mondō* (literally, questions and answers), a particular type of dialogue found in Rinzai Zen. A part of the Mahayana Buddhist tradition, they can be called ingenious Zen devices created by the practical wisdom peculiar to the Chinese. The New Testament of the Bible is the sacred scripture of Christianity. Written nearly 2,000 years ago, it is the message of salvation that Jesus Christ brought to the Jewish people. The formative processes and ideological backgrounds of the two differ: Buddhism holds that all creation is endowed with the Buddha-nature;

Christianity believes in the Three Persons in One God, as revealed by Christ, and teaches that everything in heaven and on earth has been created by this God. The one's view of history is cyclical whereas the other has a lineal view of salvation history. They differ in many other points as well. In fact, Zen koans and Christian Scripture are so utterly different that there does not seem to be the remotest possibility of finding fundamental similarities between them. I thought this for a long time and my ideas did not change even after I started to practise Zen some years ago. After returning from Germany, however, I began sincerely to devote myself to the Zen practice that I had begun previously. As I acquired a certain amount of experience in Zen, I became aware of a strange thing: I discovered that even though they differ greatly in externals, in their essentials there is a surprising resemblance between koans and Scripture.

This experience first occurred in such an unobtrusive way that I did not clearly realize it myself. When I started to do zazen (sitting meditation), I found, to begin with, that I was able to read Scripture more tranquilly and appreciate its profound meaning more readily. In the beginning I did not know why doing zazen helped me to understand the meaning of the Bible. As the experience repeated itself, however, I began to reflect on it and deduced a psychological explanation: when the mind becomes tranquil through doing zazen, the spiritual meaning of Scripture is able to penetrate to the depths of the heart. Undoubtedly doing zazen has this kind of psychological effect on the reading of Scripture, but the real reason remained concealed from me. At the time, I still did not dream that there was an internal resemblance between koans and the Bible. Later, as I participated in Zen retreats (called *sesshin*) over a period of time, I found, to my surprise, that when I returned home I could appreciate Scripture better and realize the meaning of passages which up to then had been completely incomprehensible to me, as if scales had fallen from my eyes. As this experience was repeated time and again, I began to see that koans and the Bible have something in common.

In this book I will describe, first of all, how I encountered Zen. Actually, since beginning the practice of Zen, I have

learned many things from it: complete purification of body
and soul, a way of deep contemplation, the fusion of prayer
and everyday life, as well as many other things too numerous
to mention. From among them I have chosen four which are
necessary to know in order to understand the similarities
between koans and the Bible and the characteristics that Zen
and Christian religious practice have in common. These
comprise Part I, 'Learning from Zen'. In the first section I
have also taken up several koans and Biblical passages,
touching upon their common characteristics.

Since 'body-reading Zen koans and the Bible' is the central
theme of this work, and indeed was originally considered for
its sub-title, Part II, 'Koans and the Bible', has been placed in
the middle of the book. Koans and Scripture are discussed
not only in this section, however; although the subject or
point of view may vary, this is the keynote running throughout the book. Furthermore, as I will explain in detail in Part
II, the reading of koans and Scripture with the whole 'body',
not just with the head, is the main point of this book. For
this reason I have adapted a term used by the Buddhist Saint
Nichiren, *body-reading* (*shikidoku*) into modern Japanese
(*shindoku*).

I learned Christianity by studying the catechism. Although
necessary as an introduction to the faith, the catechism alone
was inadequate to give me a deep understanding of it. It was
through the Ignatian *Spiritual Exercises* that I obtained a
deeper knowledge of the essence of Christianity and learned
how to put it into practice with my own body. Later, when I
started practising Zen, I discovered that the *Exercises* and a
Zen *sesshin* greatly resemble one another. What is more, I
think the many things I have learned from Zen have enabled
me to put new life into my practice of the *Exercises*. The
third part of the book, 'The *Spiritual Exercises* and a Zen
sesshin' came out of this personal experience.

In putting this book together, I have received the kind
help of many people. My deep indebtedness to Master
Sōgen Ōmori cannot be expressed in words. In addition, I
wish to thank from the bottom of my heart, Masters Kōun
Yamada, the late Keisan Shirozuke, and Ennō Itohara, and
the Reverend Kōsō Satō; also, my many senior and fellow

practitioners in Zen, as well as Fathers Enomiya Lassalle and Arrupe and the innumerable teachers and superiors who have guided me in Christianity. To Father William Johnston of the Institute of Oriental Religions, Sophia University, Tokyo, I am greatly indebted for his careful reading of the manuscript and many valuable suggestions. I am also grateful to the Institute of Oriental Religions, Sophia University, for financial assistance in translating the book into English. I would also like to express my sincere gratitude to Mr Ryūichi Kanda, president of Shunjū Publishing Co., for his readiness in undertaking the publishing of the Japanese version of this volume, and to Mr Mikio Hayashi, his editor-in-chief, and Mr Ryōji Ebara of the editorial staff, for carrying out the actual work involved, and to Miss Joan Rieck for her English translation. Except where indicated, quotations from *The Spiritual Exercises* of Ignatius Loyola are taken from the translation by Anthony Mottola, Image Books, New York, 1964.

Kakichi Kadowaki

Glossary

delusive passions (Sanskrit *kleśa*; Japanese *bonnō*): the mental functions which disturb the mind; illusion; worldly passions.

dōjō (J): a practice hall.

dokusan (J): a private meeting between Zen master and student in which the student's understanding is tested and the master gives direction in Zen practice.

emancipation (Skt *vimukti, vimoksa*; J *gedatsu*): freedom from the bonds of suffering and illusion.

emptiness (Skt *śūñyatā*): a term in Buddhist philosophy for the teaching that all existence is dependent on causation. Because causal factors are constantly changing, there is no static phenomenal existence; all phenomena are relative and dependent on other phenomena and therefore 'empty'. Śūñyatā should not be confused with nihilism or taken as a denial of the existence of phenomena.

gonsen koan (J): a koan that studies the words of the Zen Patriarchs and brings the student to an understanding of their deepest meaning, which he must then express in his own words.

hara (J): literally meaning the abdomen or viscera, it is also translated as mind, heart or intention. The *hara* is the physical centre of gravity in the body and also a centre of vital energy.

hosshin koan (J; Skt *dharma-kāya*): literally, *hosshin* means 'Law-Body' or 'Truth-Body'; it is the absolute nature of the Buddha-mind, the body of the highest aspect of the threefold body of the Buddha, the essence of being. The *hosshin* koans help the Zen student see more clearly into the undifferentiated realm of his own essential being, which he has realized in enlightenment.

ignorance (Skt *avidyā*; J *mumyō*): ignorance of the true nature of existence; also called delusion.

karma (Skt): the process of cause and effect; the fundamental doctrine in Buddhism that every action which is a cause will have an effect. In the same way every effect is the cause of a future resultant action.

kenshō (J): literally 'seeing into one's nature', it is the experience of enlightenment; also called *satori*.

kikan koan (J): a koan dealing with the interlockings of differentiation. By means of such a koan, a student who has seen into the undifferentiated realm of his True Self is made to return to and penetrate the differentiated realm of the everyday world.

koan (J; Chinese, *kung-an*; pronounced as two syllables in Japanese, *ko-an*): originally it meant a public case which established a legal precedent. In Zen it is a formula pointing to a universal principle of Truth. Often it takes the form of a *mondō* (question and answer) in which the Zen Master's enigmatic response to a disciple's question forces the disciple to abandon logical reasoning and come to an understanding on a deeper level of awareness. Koans are assigned to Zen students in order to bring them to enlightenment or to test and deepen their realization.

kōjō koan (J): from *kōjō jikishi* (directly pointing to the ultimate), this is the final category of koans used to clarify and deepen the insight of the advanced Zen student.

mind (J *kokoro* or *shin*): always used in this book in the Eastern sense of the word that is, the heart or spirit; it does not refer merely to the mental faculties. The word *heart* whenever it appears in the book is a translation of the Japanese *kokoro* or *shin*.

mondō (J): literally, 'question and answer', is a Zen dialogue in which the response to a question about ultimate principles of truth is one that cannot be grasped by ordinary intellection, but must be apprehended on a deeper intuitive level.

Mu (J): literally, 'no' or 'nothingness', in Zen it is another name for the True Self that transcends subject and object, affirmation and negation. As used in the koan 'Jōshu's

Dog', it is a meaningless exclamation pointing directly at the Truth, which the Zen student uses as a means to concentrate his mind and come to realization.

nantō koan (J): a koan most difficult to pass through, it develops the student's free working in differentiation and can be grasped clearly only by a student with a deep realization.

no-mind: the seeing of Reality directly without attachment to any thought or specific state of consciousness.

prajñā (Skt): True Wisdom which enables one to distinguish what is true from what is false. It is achieved in enlightenment when the discriminating consciousness has been abandoned and all dualism transcended.

religious practice (J *gyō*; Skt *caryā*): religious acts or exercises which aim at bringing one closer to the goal of enlightenment.

samādhi (Skt; J *sammai*): complete absorption and concentration of the mind in itself; the free working of no-mind transcending action and quietude.

satori (J): enlightenment; the experience of realizing one's true nature (*kenshō*); a dying to the relativistic self and rebirth as the True Self.

sesshin (J): literally, 'to collect or regulate the mind'; a period of intensive Zen practice.

zazen (J): the Zen practice of absorbing the mind in itself, while seated in the lotus posture, in an effort to awaken to the True Self.

Part I

Learning from Zen

Chapter 1

Encounter with Zen

Why does a Catholic priest practise Zen?

People often ask me this question. It seems that to the eyes of others I appear strange, but I myself am not conscious of doing anything unusual. I have simply acted according to a deep feeling that it is something I should do, and it has just naturally become something I must do. So when I am asked this question, I am at a loss for an answer. I hesitate not because I have no reason, but rather because there are so many reasons I do not know which single one would strike closest to the truth. To give a simple explanation for something one does just on the spur of the moment is hard enough, but trying to pinpoint your motive for doing something that has ripened only after the passage of many months and years, as in the case of my doing zazen, is difficult indeed. There is a long history to my encounter with Zen. I think that an account of my pilgrimage leading up to this meeting may provide some kind of answer to the above question. I hope, too, that some purpose will be served in looking back over the course by which my Zen-like education in school and my religious practice as a Christian brought me to the practice of Zen.

My first encounter with Zen began when I was in secondary school. I was not baptized as a Christian until my third year in college, so my meeting with Zen was much earlier than that with Christianity. Shizuoka Prefectural Mitsuke Middle School, in which I was enrolled, was famous for its character training. Many of the teachers were practising Zen. Thus during my five years there I was influenced both visibly and invisibly by Zen and, without knowing it, was educated according to the Zen spirit. There were some teachers of very fine character, including the well-known principal Mr Ozaki, and the man who was my fifth-year class teacher, Mr Nishi. The influence of these two men on me was so great that it determined the direction of my life. In school, the principal and teachers would join the students in manual labour, setting an example for our lives after graduation and, at the same time, cultivating our minds and bodies. It was an education aimed at instilling frugality and fortitude. Even in the middle of winter we were not allowed to wear socks in the school building or coat and gloves outside. A number of times we were taken to Zen temples by the class teacher where we would spend several days participating in training sessions. The bracing feeling of those days is still impressed on my mind. It goes without saying that this sort of secondary education played a decisive role in the formation of my personality. But, what is more important, this character training eventually led me to Christianity and finally motivated me to take up the practice of Zen.

After leaving secondary school, I became a Catholic, and three years after graduating from college, I entered the Society of Jesus. I spent two years as a novice, and during that time, I discovered that the Zen-like education I had received in secondary school was a good preparation for a Catholic novitiate. At the same time, I realized that life in a Zen monastery and a Catholic novitiate are very similar. Let me mention a few of the ways in which I have found from experience that they resemble each other.

In order to enter a Buddhist monastery, the aspiring monk must undergo severe tests. He is forced to wait at the entrance of the monastery for two days before being allowed to enter and then has to sit alone in zazen for three to five days as proof of his sincerity. Entrance to a Catholic religious order also involves a strict screening. Although I had made up my mind to enter the Society of Jesus during a retreat that I made straight after Baptism, the Society would not accept me immediately, and I had to wait for three years to enter. During that time, I visited my spiritual director every month, reported on my spiritual state and received his instruction. For two of those three years, I was made to study Latin with a group of young seminarians. I am poor at memorizing and accordingly have no aptitude for languages, so it was a very painful two years.

Novitiate in the Society of Jesus

As I mentioned above, once I entered the Society and started my period of novitiate, I was surprised to see in how many ways it resembled life in a Zen monastery. Each morning we got up at five, did exercises outdoors and, after washing, spent an hour in meditation. Another hour was spent in Mass and thanksgiving. Breakfast was at 7.30 a.m., followed by thirty minutes of cleaning. After a brief rest, we had an hour's talk by the novice master. Now, if you were to change this schedule just a little — rising at 4 a.m. instead of 5, doing zazen instead of meditation, having morning sutras instead of Mass, and a talk by the Zen master instead of the novice master — the daily schedule in a Jesuit novitiate could easily be transformed into that of a Zen monastery.

In the afternoon, we worked for an hour or two, weeding the garden, building rock steps, digging trenches, cleaning out water drains, or carrying baskets of earth, just as Zen monks do during their work periods. One time I had to scour concrete steps running up a slope of several hundred metres in the scorching sun. The job took nearly two weeks of hard labour. When I remembered the work we did as a public service during school days, however, it did not seem so difficult and I was able to throw myself into the job. The daily schedule was tightly composed of thirty-minute or one-hour units. And, like our Zen monk counterparts, we kept silence and moved as a group at the signal of a bell.

In the same fashion as a mendicant Zen monk, I have had the experience of going from door to door begging and being barked at by dogs. As one of the important activities of the novitiate, some of us spent a month helping the patients in a leprosarium while others worked in a factory in town, getting just as dirty as their fellow labourers. Another important part of our training was the eight-day and thirty-day retreats. I was struck by how much these retreats resembled Zen *sesshin* and will dwell on that point at greater length in the third part of this book. There are many other points of similarity between the novitiate and Zen religious training that could be mentioned, but I would like to proceed to the next part instead of taking time to go into them here.

After finishing two years of novitiate and three years of philosophy, I took a job teaching at the newly established Hiroshima Gakuin High School. Something happened there that I shall never forget. The father of one of the students was head of the labour bureau in the prefectural government office. This man was practising under Master Eizan Tatta and had already passed the first barrier in Zen. I was impressed by his character and felt my interest in Zen being reawakened. Just at that time, I heard that Father Enomiya Lassalle was lecturing on 'Zen and Christianity' at the Hiroshima Cathedral for World Peace. I immediately made arrangements to go with this man to hear the lecture.

Father Lassalle is a German Jesuit who has become a naturalized Japanese citizen. He was not far from the centre of the atomic bomb blast in Hiroshima, but, by some miracle, survived. After the war, he went around the world collecting donations to build a cathedral dedicated to world peace in the heart of Hiroshima. He had long been interested in the Zen method of meditation and by that time had been practising for over ten years. Many people had come to hear his talk. Standing in the pulpit, Father Lassalle told us first in fluent Japanese, about his own experience in doing zazen. He then went on to say how much it had deepened his Christian prayer. His talk, based as it was on his own experience, was very persuasive. I was deeply moved and felt a strong urge welling up in me. For a long time I had been feeling an irrepressible desire for union with God and a kind of secret premonition, perhaps, that Zen would help me realize this desire. Now Father Lassalle's talk was telling me that this was not just a premonition. I made an inner resolve that, if given the chance, I would do real Zen practice some day.

Later on, I went to Tokyo for four years of theological study. Once there, I lost no time in going to Heirin Temple in Nobidome, Saitama Prefecture, where I begged Master Keizan

Shirozuke to direct me in Zen. In those days the Catholic Church was not as tolerant of other religions as it is today, and so, unfortunately, as a seminarian I was not allowed to take part in a *sesshin*. But I often went to Heirin Temple to hear Master Keizan's sermons. Master Ennō Itohara, the present chief priest, was assistant priest at the time and taught me the practicalities of zazen, and so on. Though I did not participate in any *sesshin*, I started to sit by myself at home, doing zazen for my morning hour of meditation. Christian meditation ordinarily makes use of the reason and imagination, so when I first adopted the Zen method it felt strange. I had been accustomed, when praying, to put myself before God in an attitude of profound respect; therefore to sit with my legs folded seemed somehow disrespectful. As I made progress in doing zazen, however, I found that it suited Christian prayer very well. For the more than ten years since then, except for the period when I lived overseas, I have continued to do my Christian meditation in the Zen way.

Reforms of the Second Vatican Council

In 1962, having finished theology and a tertianship of ten months, I went to Rome to study. It happened that the Second Vatican Council was about to begin. Thus, by a stroke of good luck, I was given the opportunity to witness this historic council at close hand. The Second Vatican Council was an epoch-making event in the 2,000-year history of the Catholic Church and turned the Church in an entirely new direction. Part of that new turn in direction was a change in her attitude toward other religions. Up until then, the opinion that all other religions outside Christianity were heretical and in error had been very strong in the Church. But that thinking changed completely as a result of the Council. From the first, Christian faith has held that all men are brothers in Christ and members of the same family under God the Father. When this faith is deepened and its meaning really comes home to a Christian, he naturally feels ashamed for having had the attitude towards other religions mentioned above. It was from this that a posture of dialogue with other religions developed. God the Father, in whom we believe, desires the unity and salvation of all mankind; it is certain, therefore, that He also wants us to co-operate and consult with other religions. Furthermore, since God the Father acts in all men, he must be at work in the non-Christian religions as well. If that is true, then certainly other religions also have great worth. Reflecting on it this way, we have to admit that there is great value in the spiritual legacy transmitted and developed in these religions over many generations, and it should be studied by us Christians.

As I said, I had already secretly resolved to practice Zen; therefore this posture of dialogue in the Second Vatican Council was a great spur for me. At the same time, I realized that the impulse I had felt in the depths of my heart as I listened to Father Lassalle's talk was, without doubt, genuine and sincere.

In 1965 I returned to Japan where several fruitless years passed with no chance to practise Zen. But at last the time was ripe, and the opportunity I had been hoping for presented itself. Father Lassalle built a Catholic *zendō* (meditation hall) called Shinmeikutsu (The Cave of Divine Darkness) in Akigawa, Okutama, west of Tokyo. I promptly took part in a *sesshin* there. The man in charge of the sitting was a Mr S who had studied at Tokyo University and spent several years at a Rinzai Zen monastery. Thanks to his skill in pulling the *zendō* together, it was a very good *sesshin*.

Taking part in this *sesshin* was no more than standing at the gate of Zen, but for me it was an unforgettable experience. The following are some notes I took of a conversation I had with S after that *sesshin*.

On the last day of *sesshin*, S and I were able to have a leisurely talk. We were discussing various things when suddenly he looked very serious and, altering the tone of his voice, said, 'Since the last *sesshin* I've started to feel that something of great importance is happening here.' He spoke as though he were forcing out words that had been hidden in the depths of his being. Surprised at the intensity of his tone, I was at a loss for words for a moment. From the way that he spoke and the brightness of his eyes, I could tell that something important was going on in his mind, but had no idea what it was. Seeing the questioning look on my face, he quietly began to explain.

What he said went something like this:
'There have already been five or six *sesshin* at Shinmeikutsu. At the weekly zazen meetings on Sundays, ordinary people are in the majority, but for some strange reason, when it comes to *sesshin*, Catholic laymen and priests and sisters always predominate. Among them is a nurse who comes all the way from Nara for every *sesshin*. She does extra night duty so that she can get a few days off and comes up to Tokyo on the night train. At Shinmeikutsu she is called Lady Tesshū, after the famous Tesshū Yamaoka who used to gallop on horseback from Tokyo to Mishima in order to take part in *sesshin* at Ryūtakuji Temple. At any rate, the zeal of the Catholic participants can be accounted for, I think, by the fact that they have at last found in Zen something which they had given up hope of finding anywhere else. If that were all, it probably wouldn't be so surprising. But recently I've begun to notice that there is more to it than that. I don't know how to say it properly, but I've been seized with the conviction, would you call it? – a sure presentiment that there is something deep in the souls of Catholics that harmonizes perfectly with Zen meditation and that something too deep to fathom comes out of this.' (*Seiki [Century]* 1971, July)

I was to learn later from personal experience, part of which I will describe in this book, that S's presentiment was correct. Also, for the past five years I have been conducting Zen-style retreats for Catholic Sisters and have seen many of them experience the same thing, almost like a chain reaction.

Later on, I was to have the good fortune to receive the direction of many Zen masters, and each encounter was valuable beyond expression. Unfortunately, there is not room to tell about them all here.

Chapter 2

Learning through the body

Gutei holds up a finger (*Mumonkan*, Case 3)

If your right eye causes you to sin, pluck it out
and throw it away (Matthew 5:29)

Religious practice (Sanskrit caryā) — the Eastern tradition

I have learned many things from Zen, but one of the most
wonderful is to have become aware of the importance of the
body in religious life. Up until now, whether in prayer,
repentance, or reading the Bible, Christianity has attached
little importance to the body. The way of Zen is in striking
contrast to this. As Dōgen Zenji says in the *Bendōwa*
(Discourses on Buddhist Practice), 'Proper sitting is the true
gate to the practice of Zen.' Learning through the body is a
fundamental of Zen. It is a way which proceeds 'from the
body to the mind' by first adjusting one's posture in a proper
sitting position, regulating the breath and composing the
mind. We can call it a method of practising with the whole
'body'.

Christianity took the opposite direction as it developed in
the West. The Western way is to first reflect rationally, make
a judgment, will to do something, and finally use the body to
carry out the act. This way of proceeding can be called 'from
reason to the body'.

Such characterizations of Zen and Western Christianity
smack of over-simplification, but in general, I think that we
can say this is the case. Actually, the 'body' does have a
profound relation to the central thought of Christianity, as I
will discuss later, and it is highly valued in many respects.

Yet, I think it can be said that as it developed in the West, Christianity did not sufficiently reflect on the 'body' or discover that 'from the body to the mind' was unsurpassed as a way leading to a deep religious experience. Under the strong influence of Greek thought, Christianity inclined toward rationalism and generally followed the way of 'from reason to the body'. Accordingly, it had no religious practice (*Sanskrit caryā*) that perfected the spirit through the training of the body.

In the East, on the contrary, such practice developed remarkably as a way of religious training. Indian Yoga, the *dhyana* (meditation) of primitive Buddhism, the *shikan* meditative exercises of Tendai Buddhism, the three secret rituals of Esoteric Buddhism, recitation of the Nembutsu in Jodō and Shin Buddhism, invoking the name of Amida Buddha and the sacred title of the Lotus Sutra in Nichiren Buddhism, Shugendō's mountain asceticism — all are forms of *caryā*. Zen took its rise from the Yoga tradition of more than four or five thousand years ago and, in the process of transmission from India to Japan by way of China, created an extremely refined mental and physical way of practice. In one sense, I think it is not an exaggeration to say that this way is the finest flower of Eastern culture. The more proficient I become in zazen, the more deeply I feel this. It is because I am experiencing with my own body how wonderfully the practice of Zen can change a person. For example, when I first began to do zazen, I felt as though the following lines by Mumon pertained to some distant dreamland:

> Then all of a sudden, you will break through the barrier, astonishing the heavens and shaking the earth. It will be just as though you had snatched the great sword of General Kan. If you meet the Buddha, you will kill him. If you meet an ancient master, you will kill him. Though you stand on the brink of life and death, you will enjoy the great freedom. In the six realms and the four modes of birth, you will live in the *samādhi* of innocent delight (*Mumonkan*, Case 1).

It is strange, but as I make progress in my Zen practice, the state of consciousness described in this passage no longer seems so distant. Although I cannot say I have achieved the 'great freedom', I have come to the point where I feel I can face death without anxiety or struggle. That I have changed in this short period of time is certain, but even I am surprised at the way in which I have changed.

Now, how is it that such a wonderful power lies hidden in the way of Zen? Zazen is extremely simple. It is just a matter of sitting upright with proper posture, regulating your breathing and composing your mind. How, then, can it change a person so drastically? It really is a mystery. Actually, man's True Self has astounding power; he just does not know how to tap this enormous force with which he is intrinsically endowed. I believe that the way of Zen is unsurpassed in bringing this energy to bloom. The secret is to devote every ounce of strength in your entire 'body' to doing it. This can be explained in part by referring to the phenomenology of the 'body'.

The phenomenology of the 'body'

Like Zen, modern phenomenology of the 'body' starts from the unity of body and mind. According to this phenomenology, 'body' refers to the entire person, the unity of mind and body. It is the 'body-as-subject'. A person is not something that has a body. *Person* means a body animated by a soul; it is the 'body' itself. Therefore it is correct to say that a person is a 'body'. The word *soma* (body) in the Bible obviously refers to the whole person. When we look at a beautiful view out of the window, the thing that sees the view is not the eye, or the soul, but the whole body. In such a case, if we say, 'I'm looking at the view', this 'I' is unconsciously interpreted as the 'I' at the core of one's consciousness, in a word, one's soul. This is a subtle misapprehension which changes the reality slightly. Actually, the 'I' that is seeing is not merely the soul, not merely the body, but the unity of body and soul that is my whole self. Even if you were to separate them, when you look at a view the principal role is played by the seeing eyes, so it would be more correct to say that it is your body that is seeing. The same thing can be said not only about seeing, but about all the actions of daily life. Whether hearing, talking, walking, eating, sleeping, writing or reading, the main actor is not the soul but the body. Let us reflect a bit on the phenomenon of speech. When I speak to another person, it is not our souls or minds that face each other. Rather, it is my body and the body of the other that are conversing together. The body of the other person turns its ears to my words and opens its mouth to address me. At the same time that he becomes involved with me by these acts, he is also relating to other people, the world and to God. Here there is something I would especially like to call the reader's attention to: when you sincerely turn your body to face another person and attentively listen to what he is saying, even if his body does not utter a word, it is already speaking to you.

As a matter of fact, human speech does not primarily depend on words. The whole body speaks first. It is not until you have 'body language' that oral dialogue can take place. The term *body language* does not refer here to motions of the hands or body, but to a language that exists even without such gestures. Heidegger says that to the extent that *Dasein* exists, it is speech (*Rede*). He does not take up the physical nature of *Dasein* at a deep level, but it is obvious that by it he means the whole person. As I said above, I interpret the body to be the whole person, so that if there is a body, it is already speaking. This idea is developed, I think, by taking Heidegger's real meaning into account.

At any rate, there is no doubt that my body is speaking even when I am not doing anything. And this speech has a connection with other people, the world and with God. Furthermore, each act or word that comes from my body is given direction and meaning by my 'body language'. If it did not exist, then no matter how eloquently I were to speak, I would not really be saying anything. A person who is determined not to reveal his true feelings, for example, may become quite eloquent in order to hide them, but in actuality, it is as if he were not speaking at all.

Each movement of the body changes it, giving it an increasingly living 'form'. The 'form' it takes is the articulation of the 'language' of the body and makes the expression of that 'language' clearer. To the extent that personality is formed by actions, the whole life of the person becomes impressed on and manifested by his bodily 'form'. We can say that a person's 'form' is speaking of his personality.

The koan 'Gutei holds up a finger'

There is a Zen koan which has taught me much about 'body language'. It is 'Gutei holds up a finger'.

> Whenever Master Gutei was asked [about Zen], he simply held up a finger. He had a young attendant who was asked by a visitor, 'What kind of teaching does your master give?' The boy raised up a finger. Gutei heard about this and cut off the boy's finger with a knife. As the attendant ran off screaming with pain, Gutei called to him. When he turned his head, Gutei held up his finger. The boy was suddenly enlightened (*Mumonkan*, Case 3).

As I said above, a person's 'form' speaks of his personality. To the observer who has eyes to see, the body of a deeply enlightened person tells of that person's lofty state of realization. When Master Gutei was asked about the secret principles of Zen, he surely responded with his entire body and mind. Nevertheless, his questioners must have been taken aback, for his answer was the unexpected holding up of a finger. With the raising of his finger, Gutei perfectly manifested his True Self. If his questioners had had eyes to see, they would have perceived the True Self the master presented in this surprising action. But conversely, for a person without an eye, Gutei's gesture must have been absolutely incomprehensible.

The important point here is the difference between Gutei's action and the attendant's imitation of it. In Gutei's case, it is a manifestation of his vigorous and unrestricted state of realization, whereas in the case of the boy it is nothing more than a mimicry of his master. Another thing to notice is the skillfulness Gutei shows in his harsh treatment of the boy; it should be seen as an expression of his compassion for him.

The boy must have screamed with all his might from the pain. Putting his whole body and soul into crying out, he forgot himself and became pain itself. When a person becomes completely absorbed in something, the True Self, which has been sleeping inside of him, silently reveals itself. Master Gutei could not let this golden opportunity pass. Immediately calling the boy back, he thrust up a finger in the air. The state of mind of the young attendant must have been like that of a chick about to hatch from the egg. By means of the uplifted finger, into which Gutei had put his entire body and soul, he was able to break through his shell and leap out into the world of freedom. This was truly 'simultaneous picking and pecking' (a Zen expression which refers to the minds of master and disciple coming into contact, just as a hen, from the outside, and a chick, from the inside, peck at the same point on the eggshell to break it open). We see here that a great person like Gutei says more with his 'body' than with countless words of preaching.

Composure of body, breath, and mind

The above should give the reader some idea of what is meant by *caryā*, religious practice that disciplines the mind and heart via the body. Just try, for example, sitting upright with proper posture. You will see that straightening up corrects not only your physical posture but also your entire 'body', your whole person. It is a strange person whose mind is not composed by the straightening of his body. When you sit up properly, your mind becomes orderly. Conversely, when you sit in a slouch, your mind slouches too.

The same thing can be said in regard to breathing. To regulate your breath is to compose your mind. If you breathe slowly and deeply from the abdomen, your mind becomes relaxed and tranquil. If, at the same time, you employ the methods of composing the mind used in Zen, it also becomes unified and concentrated. There are various ways of regulating the mind. When the koan 'Mu' is used, it means simply to recite 'Mu' mentally with each exhalation. The important thing is to put your whole mind and heart into this one act. 'Do it with every ounce of your energy,' my Master, Sōgen Ōmori, always says, 'as if with "Mu" you were pushing through

your anus, your cushion, and right through to the other side
of the world!' As this indicates, one's total mental and
physical energy must be mobilized. This, of course, involves
posture, breathing, one's energy, and all the activity of the
mind, as well as a great faith and a courage that reach to the
deepest recesses of the heart. I would like to point out in
passing that faith plays an important role. In Zen, the 'great
root of faith' is the belief that man lives by the life of
Buddha. In Christianity, we believe that not only do we live
by the life of God, but that the Three Persons in One God
dwell in us. When a Christian does zazen, he must penetrate
into the essence of this belief. The stronger this faith is, the
more the mind is concentrated and the easier it is to be
emancipated from egoism. Thus zazen not only demands
physical activity such as regulation of posture and breathing,
but it also brings into play the entire working of the mind,
including its unconscious energies. And because the thrust
of the person's total mental and physical capacities is concentrated in this single ball of 'Mu', it naturally results in an
explosive burst of astounding energy. When this happens,
mind, breath, and body become a harmonious whole, and
the person's True Self leaps forth and is recognized.

From this we can see that zazen is an unsurpassed way of
tapping the tremendous power with which all men are
intrinsically endowed.

When I was able to pass the koan 'Gutei holds up a finger',
I was reminded of these hard words of Christ in the Bible:

> If your right eye causes you to sin, pluck it out and throw it away;
> it is better that you lose one of your members than that your
> whole body be thrown into hell. And if your right hand causes you
> to sin, cut it off and throw it away; it is better that you lose one of
> your members than that your whole body go into hell (Matthew
> 5:29-30).

This passage shows a severity in Christ that approaches
cruelty, but we should not overlook the great compassion
that is hidden behind the harsh words.

Ordinarily the passage is interpreted to mean that Jesus is
well aware of the terrible torment that awaits the sinner in
hell; he says, therefore, wouldn't it be better to lose one or

even both of your hands than to go through such suffering?
Even though this interpretation is probably not wrong, I
think it misses the deeper significance of Christ's words. If
they are merely an appeal to people's rational self-interest,
telling them to consider which is more advantageous, it is
simply the preaching of some second or third-rate religious
teacher.

I see, instead, in these harsh words of Christ, the pulsating
of his love. Love transcends self-interest. Was there calcula-
tion in Master Gutei's cutting off of the boy's finger? Or was
it compassion that compelled him to cut it off with such
quick resourcefulness? The answer is clear. We should not fail
to notice that when Gutei cut off the finger, he and the boy
were not separate beings, in opposition to each other. The
boy's finger was, at the same time, his finger. The enlightenment of Zen is to realize with the 'body' that all things have
the same source, and that the self is one with everything
else. In cutting off the boy's finger, Gutei was cutting off
his own finger.

The same thing can be said about Jesus, in the highest
sense of the word. When he exclaimed, 'If your eye causes
you to sin, pluck it out and throw it away,' he was not
thinking of 'you' and himself as separate entities. 'Your eye'
is Jesus's eye. To pluck out your eye is to pluck out the eye
of Jesus. This is because love binds all people together and
makes it impossible for a person to think something, anything at all, is unrelated to him. A sermon given by a German
in the Middle Ages, the Christian mystic Meister Eckhart,
helps us understand this better. In it, he explains the mystery
of love with a moving parable:

> A certain young nobleman married a woman of matchless beauty,
> and they lived a happy life together. Then they were suddenly struck
> by misfortune. The beautiful young wife lost her eyesight and,
> overcome with grief, fell into great despondency. Fearing that she
> would lose her husband's love, she grew weary of this world and
> longed for death. On seeing his wife's suffering, the nobleman drew
> his sword and gouged out both of his eyes with it. Then he said to
> his wife, 'Don't grieve that way. I will never desert you. My love for
> you will never change: as proof of it, I have gouged out my eyes.
> Now I, too, can no longer see anything.'

Jesus has this spirit of love to a greater degree than anyone else. Or perhaps it is better to say that Jesus is the source of this kind of love. The best expression of it is in his death on the cross. The 'form' of Christ dying on the cross to save mankind speaks of his infinite love. Christians who have learned 'body language' should be able to understand something of what his dead 'body' on the cross is saying to us. When I passed the koan 'Gutei holds up a finger', I felt as though I had been given keener ears with which to hear the 'body language' of the crucified Jesus.

Chapter 3

Religious conversion

What is heard as 'do no evil' is the True Dharma
of Buddhism (Dōgen)

Repent and believe in the Gospel (Mark 1:15)

Do no evil

Another thing I have learned from Zen is the complete
purification of the 'body' through composure of body,
breath and mind. Persons who learn about Zen only from
books often have the mistaken notion that sin is not an
issue in Zen and that purification and conversion are ignored.
Such persons will no doubt be surprised when I say that Zen
has taught me what complete purification is. For those who
are earnestly seeking the Way through Zen practice, to 'do no
evil' is a matter of course or, rather, it is the first step of
practice.

In the chapter entitled 'Do No Evil' of the *Shōbōgenzō*
(The Eye and Treasury of the True Law), Dōgen Zenji writes:

> In studying the exquisite knowledge of the Supreme Wisdom, we
> hear the teachings of a qualified Master and sometimes read the
> sutras. Then at first 'do no evil' is heard. If 'do no evil' is not heard,
> it is not the true Dharma of Buddha, but the teaching of the devil.
> You should know that to hear 'do no evil' is the true Dharma.
> Ordinary man does not contrive the thought to 'do no evil' by
> himself. When he hears the preaching of the Wisdom of Buddha it is
> naturally heard as this. What is heard in this way is the expression in
> words of the Supreme Wisdom. Therefore they are already the words
> of Wisdom. Hearing them, one is pulled by their force and moved to

19

neither desire nor to evil. And when evil is no longer done, this is the immediate actualization of the power of religious practice. The person who does this kind of practice, even though he may live in conditions where it is easy to commit evil or may associate with evil-doing people, will never commit evil.

These words of Master Dōgen leave no doubt that Zen practice involves the avoidance of sin. When the practice of a great man of Zen is perfected, 'the power of spiritual discipline is realized at once' and he is purified to the extent of becoming incapable of evil acts.

It is true that the consciousness of sin is disregarded in Zen whereas Christianity teaches that all men are sinners. On the surface these two views seem completely contrary, and on the basis of this apparent disparity, some persons conclude that Zen and Christianity are fundamentally different. Certain Christians, hearing that Zen disregards the consciousness of sin, consider it to be the teaching of the devil. Then there are Zen practitioners who see Christians being tormented by a sense of sin and call Christianity an evil way. Both opinions are based on serious misunderstandings that come from not having an eye that sees the whole. It is like looking at part of an elephant's leg and mistaking it for the whole animal, and then judging the worth of the elephant by your impressions of the leg. My teacher, Master Sōgen Ōmori, never ceases to stress that in order to judge things properly you need a discerning eye. It goes without saying that a person who wants to understand religion, which pursues a knowledge of man's ultimate concern, must have an eye of the highest power. A discerning eye can intuitively grasp with one glance first the whole, then the parts of the whole, and then returning to the whole, see the relation between it and its parts as well as the relations between the various parts. But this discerning eye cannot be obtained through intellectual discipline alone. It is only when you throw your entire body and soul into religious practice and are purified in your whole person that you are given this kind of wisdom.

We should not forget that in both Zen and Christianity numerous teachers have undergone this long and difficult practice, nor should we make rash judgments on just a smattering of information. If we really want to understand a religion, there is no other way than to walk ourselves the austere path that its founder and patriarchs followed and acquire a discerning eye capable of grasping it whole.

The doctrine of original sin

What Christianity is trying to teach by its doctrine of original sin is, in fact, also recognized in Zen and used as the starting point of its practice. Since my aim in this book is not to make a comparison of doctrine, but to bring together and examine what I have learned from my experience with both religions, I will not go into doctrinal comparisons here. However, I would like to explain a little about the thought that forms the basis of religious practice.

Both Christianity and Zen recognize and take as the starting point of their religious discipline the human reality that Buddhism calls delusive passion (Sanskrit *kleśa*), i.e., those mental functions which disturb the mind and heart such as covetousness, anger, ignorance, arrogance, doubt and false views. In Christian terminology they are called the seven capital sins of pride, greed, and so forth, which are deeply embedded in the human heart as a result of original sin. We know them to be a reality from our own experience, and both Zen and Christianity aim at liberation from them. (Incidentally, what is called original sin in Christianity cannot be known from human experience; it can only be known through divine revelation. Empirically we can only know the effects of original sin such as the capital sins, sickness, war, death, and so on.)

Christianity says that these passions are a result of man's alienation from his source. When man rebelled against God, the source of all creation, he not only went against what he was originally meant to be, but a cleft appeared between himself and others and himself and the whole universe. According to Buddhist teaching, the origin of delusive passion is ignorance; that is, man has lost sight of his Primal Face (Buddha-nature). Because of this ignorance, man not only offends against his True Self, but he thinks of all things as dualistically opposed. Viewing things in terms of subject and object, good and bad, being and non-being, he is deluded and tortured by his passions.

The teachings of Zen and Christianity are very dissimilar, but can we not see a correspondence here in terms of their basic structure? I find two main points of similarity between them.

First, both agree that the origin of delusive passions is a falling away from the true source of the self, and that this is a fall from man's original state. To be sure, their opinions diverge in regard to the problem of establishing where man's source is; there is also a subtle difference between them as to whether or not the fall was due to a grave offence on the part of man. But here the similarities are more important than the discrepancies. As I said before, I am examining what I have learned from my practice of Zen. From the point of view of religious practice, the above similarity has a decisive meaning: since both hold similar ideas about the origin of the passions, their method of emancipation from them (in other words, the way of purification) is also the same, as I shall discuss below.

The second point of similarity is that both consider the result of this fall to be opposition between the self and others and between the self and the universe (called 'dualistic opposition' in Buddhism).

Repentance (metanoia)

Even more significant than the similarity between Christian and Zen thought regarding the origin of the passions is the structural resemblance of their ideas on the way to be emancipated from them.

In Christianity, the first thing necessary for purification is change of heart (*metanoia*). The Greek word *metanoia* is usually translated as repentance, but it has a deeper meaning. The Old Testament mainly preaches a simple turning away from sin. Even there, a return to the merciful bosom of the Father is ultimately demanded, but the emphasis is on fleeing from one's sins of the past. In contrast to this, the *metanoia* of the New Testament has the meaning of positively facing forward. At the beginning of his missionary work, 'Jesus came into Galilee, preaching the gospel of God, and saying, "The time is fulfilled, and the kingdom of God is at hand; repent *(metonoeite)* and believe in the gospel."' (Mark 1:14-15).

It is clear from the context of the sentence that the word 'repent' is directed forward towards 'believe in the gospel'. The reason man must repent is not because he has sinned in the past. According to the account in Matthew, Jesus began his preaching with the words, 'Repent, for the kingdom of heaven is at hand' (4:17). Here it is stated clearly that one must repent because 'the kingdom of heaven is at hand'. Of course, this repentance will include a deep remorse for sin, but the weight of the emphasis is on the turning of the whole person toward the kingdom of God. Even if he has not committed any sin, man, in this sense, must still make a complete conversion. Conversion is not just the puny act of repenting for the sins of the past: it is to turn in the direction of an entirely new reality, the 'kingdom of God', and throw oneself into creating a new way of life.

Looking at it this way, we see that for Christians the first thing to be aimed at in purification is not, as is generally thought, repentance for sin, but a turning of one's whole mind and body in the direction of God our Source. Since the origin of the delusive passions lies in separation from God, the true source of everything, it is obvious that to be completely liberated from the passions, man must return to that source.

The second step required in purification is reconciliation with others and with the universe. This step is even demanded naturally by the first step. The relation between the two is clearly revealed in the following words of Christ's Sermon on the Mount.

You have heard that it was said, 'You shall love your neighbour and hate your enemy.' But I say to you, love your enemies and pray for those who persecute you, so that you may be sons of your Father who is in heaven; for he makes his sun rise on the evil and on the good, and sends rain on the just and on the unjust (Matthew 5:43-45).

Returning to the source

Among the Jews of that time it was generally held that one should love his neighbour and hate his enemies, but Jesus says, 'Love your enemies'. The reason we must love neighbour and enemy without distinction is because our Father in heaven, the source of all creation, loves both the evil and the good without distinction. We are all children of the same Heavenly Father; thus it stands to reason that we should not be hostile towards each other. If a person has a conversion of heart and returns to the Father his Origin, becoming a child of God, opposition between himself and other people and things will disappear naturally. Is it not clear, then, that the second step of purification is inherently demanded by the first?

The word 'purification' is not used in Zen, but there is a corresponding term: emancipation (Japanese *gedatsu*). How is emancipation brought about in Zen? Interestingly, like Christian purification, it involves two stages. First, having united the whole mind and body in doing 'Mu', one awakens to his Primal Face. This can be described as the overthrowing of ignorance and returning to the true source of the self. It is the realization that all creation has the same root. But even with this *kenshō* (literally, seeing into one's nature), the self is still in opposition to others and to worldly phenomena. The person has not yet become completely free of a dualistic outlook. The second step of emancipation, therefore, is to get rid of dualistic relativism in all its aspects.

The first step is carried out through the passing of the *Hosshin* (*Dharmakāya*) koans (koans which help us get an insight into the undifferentiated realm of our True Nature or *Dharmakāya*). The second step is brought about through the passing of several kinds of koans including the *kikan* (dealing with the complex interlockings of differentiation), *gonsen* (penetrating the innermost meaning of difficult words of the Zen Patriarchs and expressing them in your own words), *nantō* (most difficult to pass through), and *kōjō* (directly pointing to the ultimate) koans. The second step, we should not forget, is carried out while deepening the first. Thus an accomplished Master will weave the *Dharmakāya* koans together with the koans of the second step in giving them to a disciple and deepen the first step of the purification process by making the disciple return again and again to the true source of the self. Also, since the koans of the second step can basically be solved only by returning even more deeply to the Original Self, the second step of emancipation is something that flows naturally out of the first.

Thus we see that the practice of purification has essentially the same structure in Zen and Christianity. But, as I said above, the Christianity that developed in the West generally takes the way of 'from reason to the body', and the Christian method of purification has followed the same way. Zen, on the contrary, takes the path of 'from the body to the mind'. Anyone who actually practises both ways will realize that the latter is superior to the rationalistic method of Western Christianity. I would like to leave to the next chapter an account of how Zen taught me the method of complete purification and my theorizing about why the way of learning through both mind and body is so excellent.

On the way without leaving home

Let us look at the words of Christ quoted above once again and examine Christian purification at its ultimate point. This should help us understand what kind of purification Christ wants of us. 'Jesus came into Galilee, preaching the gospel of God, and saying, "The time is fulfilled, and the kingdom of God is at hand; repent, and believe in the gospel" ' (Mark 1:14-15).

We cannot say we understand this sacred passage if we have only an intellectual grasp of its meaning. Really to read it is to hear and follow this call of Jesus with our whole person. In order to do this we must first realize with our 'bodies' that it is an agonizing plea on which Christ has staked his life. And until we hurl our whole selves into the kingdom of God and dwell in it mind and body, we will not be able to say that we have perfectly responded to Christ's invitation. We have not truly entered the kingdom of God if what Paul calls the 'sin which dwells in us' (Romans 7:20) is still nesting undisturbed in the bottom of our hearts.

There are differences of opinion as to whether from the beginning of his missionary life Jesus really desired this kind of fundamental conversion from man. Some think he did not expect it from everyone. But I believe it is an undeniable fact that the conversion that Christ desired, and for which he was ready to die on the cross, was a conversion of the whole person, a thorough-going repentance. If this is admitted, to say that what he is ultimately asking of man in this passage is faith can only be called a shallow understanding of the Bible. The deeper interpretation is that what he really desired was complete conversion. But one who only interprets it that way still cannot be said to have really read the Bible. Until you actually carry out a thorough repentance with your whole 'body', as was described above, and enter the kingdom of God totally, making it your true home, your reading of the Bible will still be incomplete.

There is a famous expression in Zen: 'On the way without leaving home.' Life is a journey and, in that sense, man is always on the way. But the person who has realized the Primal Face of his True Self never leaves home. He is able to be on a journey while having, at the same time, the peace of mind he experiences in his own home. This Zen phrase is extolling such a state of enlightenment.

If we Christians awaken with our entire 'bodies' to the fact that we are already in the kingdom of God, we will have achieved the state of always living in our beloved 'home', even while we are on the way to the perfection of the kingdom of God. That 'home' is the one in which our merciful Heavenly Father lives together with us. If this is admitted, then, in the true sense of the word, isn't the 'good news' Jesus proclaimed the news that the kingdom of God is our 'home'?

Chapter 4

Purification of the 'body'

Transcending the deep-rootedness of delusive
passions and original sin

The 'body' is not a tool of the soul

In the preceding chapter, I discussed the complete purification of the 'body' that I learned from Zen. I explained how,
in spite of the fact that Zen and Christianity differ greatly
on the theoretical level regarding certain points of purification and conversion, in basic structure they are very similar.
In this chapter I would like to tell more concretely how the
way of Zen is useful in the purification of the 'body'.

As I have said, up to now religious practice in Christianity
has taken the way of 'from reason to the body'. The method
of purification has been no exception. The way of Western
Christianity is to overcome disturbing passions through
reason and volition: by self-examination one becomes aware
of self-love and self-centredness and then tries to change by
means of the will. The supplementary means of physical
austerities and the curbing of desires are also employed in
the purification process, but they are never more than supplementary measures and fail to take the whole 'body' into
consideration. Here I would like to call the reader's attention
to the important distinction between a means and a way.

A means is considered good if it is effective in achieving an
end, and bad if it is not. It has no value of itself; its worth is
decided in relation to the end. The relation between means
and end is important in present-day life which is conducted
according to a pragmatic and utilitarian philosophy. Yet this

philosophy can never solve man's fundamental problem. That is to say, it is impossible to deal with the relations between parent and child, brother and sister, friend and friend, or teacher and student, in terms of a means to an end. Much less can such a concept solve the various problems between religions. In the same way, the physical body cannot be thought of as a means for the soul. Even Aristotle did not consider it to be so. He held that body and soul are both constituent principles of the person, so difficult to separate that they can be said to be substantially united in the whole; the corporal body is equal to the soul as a principle which constitutes the real essence of the person. Much less does Christianity look down on the body; to consider the body as a means is not the true thought of the Church. By imperceptible degrees, however, stress has been placed more and more on the superiority of the soul, so that the mistaken notion of the body as a means has at times crept into Christian thinking. And with the added contamination of modern rationalism, even religion has come to be used by some as a utilitarian means to an end.

This is by no means happening only in the West: the same thing is also blatantly being done in Japan. A typical example is the way the Japanese New Religions effectively use promises of worldly gain or the cure of illness as a means of propagating the faith. The promotion of zazen by business management, as a means of attaining mental stability in employees, is another example. Zazen is definitely not a means. To think of it as a means to enlightenment is the first step in the corruption of Zen. Dōgen Zenji says, 'Proper sitting is the true gate to the practice of Zen.' A gate is not a means. While belonging to the house, it connects the outside world to the inside of the house. We should not call zazen a means, therefore, but a Way. This Way, however, is both the journey to the goal and the place where step by step the goal is already realized. We would have to say the same thing about the physical austerities and curbing of desire mentioned above, and other religious practices such as mendicancy and labour.

Deficiencies in Western religious practice

Now, even in the 'from reason to the body' way of religious practice in Western Christianity, the corporal body is not primarily thought of as a means. But when reason plays the predominant role, the flesh is apt to be viewed instrumentally or the importance of the 'body' disregarded. For example, in the past when a Christian was troubled with evil desires or doubts about the faith and went to a spiritual director for help with the problem, he was usually told something like the following: you are being tried; now, more than ever, you must persevere, arousing a spirit of deep faith and believing from the bottom of your heart that God will never abandon you, even in the midst of trial. As long as your will is strong, you will never be defeated by passion or unbelief.

Such advice is not wrong, and for a person of great spiritual strength, it is probably effective. But the person whose will is not so strong is usually unable to carry it out. Furthermore, this advice ignores the fact that the mind and body are interrelated, and so it merely becomes a spiritual treatise.

The truth is that human passions nest in the bottom of the heart and cannot be uprooted by reason or willpower alone. This point can be considered from three aspects.

First, we are not able to control our bodies as we please merely by the use of reason or willpower. This will be clear if we think about the case of two things which are quite unrelated: physical passions and sports. A person who has done some skiing and then learns how to do the Christiana or the Wedeln from a book will experience great frustration when he tries to make his body master them. How much more difficult it is to control the physical passions, which are so deeply bound up with the body, through reason or willpower. We are arrogant if we think we can.

Second, as Freud's concept of the unconscious and Jung's collective unconscious clearly demonstrate, it is impossible to manage our feelings through conscious activity. Emotional complexes are buried deep in the heart and one cannot become aware of them by ordinary rational self-reflection. To be cured of such complexes, even by psychoanalysis, usually requires a great deal of patience and at least several years of commuting to the psychiatrist's office.

In the third place, there is the additional problem of vices or bad habits. These cannot be cured by reason or willpower alone, either. The case of Tesshū Yamaoka (1836-88) is a good example of this. Yamaoka was a famous Japanese swordsman and calligrapher, as well as a great man of Zen. At the age of 42, he started working on the koan contained in the verse on the fourth of Tozan's Five Ranks, 'The arrival at mutual integration':

> When two blades cross points
> There's no need to withdraw.
> The master's swordsman
> Is like the lotus blooming in the fire.
> Such a man has in and of himself
> A heaven-soaring spirit.*

After three years Yamaoka finally penetrated the koan and came to a deep enlightenment. His calligraphy *Dragon and Tiger*, written immediately afterward, is completely different from anything he had ever done before. As Master Sōgen Ōmori says, this calligraphy has 'a vigour that seems to pierce the heavens. It overflows with the powerful feeling of a fierce, unapproachable tiger, and its lines dance like a leaping dragon. . . . Clear and vivid, it has a tinge of the unfathomable' (*Sho to Zen* [Calligraphy and Zen], Tokyo, Shunjūsha, 1973, p.94). Before that, Yamaoka had escaped death several times during the chaos of the Meiji Restoration and had accomplished the great work of surrendering Edo palace without bloodshed. But even in him, there remained illusive tendencies (Sanskrit *vāsarā*, the impressions or results of past deeds on the personality which remain as inclinations toward the passions), and it is said that he was still burdened with dualistic concepts. Then in the spring of his forty-ninth year, while gazing at some flowers in the garden, he was finally able to 'radically cut off life and death'. He had spent four years after his first enlightenment mentally and physically learning the Way through swordsmanship and Zen. If it took the great Tesshū Yamaoka this long, how much longer will it

---

*Translated by Isshu Miura and Ruth Fuller Sasaki in *Zen Dust*, New York, Harcourt, Brace and World, 1966, p.71.

take us ordinary people? The residual dregs of complexes
that have accumulated in our hearts over the years cannot
be removed in a day.

The deep-rootedness of illusive tendencies

In order to understand the Way of Zen, I would like to
discuss the problem of the illusive tendencies in more detail.
There are two causes for the inveterateness of these unpurified
elements. Bad habits are not only concerned with the mind;
they permeate the entire 'body'. They involve not only what
in psychological terms is called the subconscious or the
collective subconscious, but also extend to a much deeper
and broader sphere. I expressed this fact by saying they permeate the entire 'body'. As was mentioned in the previous
chapter, the word 'body' stands for the whole person as seen
from its physical nature. It covers both the conscious and the
subconscious and includes everything that goes beyond them.
The 'body' encompasses the 'eight kinds of consciousness' of
Buddhism and of course the 'root of evil' in Christianity, as
well as the effects of karma and original sin, which go beyond
the level of individual acts of right and wrong. From the
religious point of view, illusive tendencies are related to all of
these and are therefore far beyond the power of reason and
will. It is obvious that since they concern the whole 'body',
unless we work on the problem of purifying the 'body',
there can be no solution.

The second reason that illusive tendencies are so ingrained
is that the passions are distortions, not only of the physical
desires and the flesh, but also of the reason and will themselves. We generally think of egoism, for example, as the use
of everything and everyone for one's personal advantage. But
it is not only that. The activities of the reason and will are
themselves given over to egoism so that it is difficult to
become aware of it, no matter how much a person reflects on
himself. That is why they say in Zen, 'You don't notice the
smell of your own pee' (*Hekigan-roku*, Case 77). That is also
why after *kenshō*, you are burdened with thoughts about
having had it, and it is easy to stoop to the level of bragging

about your own accomplishments. The Buddhist teaching
that says ignorance is the source of all illusions is also referring to this fact. There is a blind spot in what we think of as
the bright light of reason. This is ignorance (Sanskrit *avidyā*).
It is clear that we cannot break free of it by reason and willpower alone. The more we try to do so, the stronger our
egotism becomes, and the less we are able to escape from
ourselves.

Then, what should you do? There is no other way than to
die the Great Death, thereby raising the state of your realization and coming to a higher wisdom which transcends both
reason and will. Dying the Great Death does not mean to die
to the self ideologically. It means to put your whole body
and soul into dying to your self and to be born again into an
absolutely new life. Then a higher dimension will break open
and you will attain a state of lofty wisdom and unrestricted
freedom of activity. And if this isn't the aim of Zen practice,
then what is?

Making the whole body an eye

In the previous chapter, I described at some length how zazen
composes the 'body' and releases the enormous energy
hidden in it. You aim at the Great Death of the entire 'body'
by mobilizing posture, breath, and energy. Along with this, it
is necessary to have a great root of faith, a great ball of
doubt, and a great tenacity of purpose that reach to the
deepest recesses of the mind. When you have penetrated the
Great Death, you will awaken to your Primal Face and realize
the essential nature of the Self, which is the common root of
all things. This is indeed the *prajñā* wisdom which transcends
reason and will. When the 'body' has been illumined, ordered,
and unified by this wisdom, for the first time you are able to
'drop off the mind and body of self and others'. At the
moment this happens, all traces of the illusive tendencies are
completely extinguished.

But because, for the two reasons noted above, illusive
tendencies permeate the entire 'body', it is impossible to
eradicate the bad habits of the whole 'body' or to cut out the

root of ignorance by just one *kenshō* experience. And even though one *kenshō* opens the mind's eye, its light is too weak to extend through the whole 'body' nor does it illuminate the darkness of ignorance in the core of the mind. But it should have become clear from the explanation of the 'body' given thus far, that putting the whole body and soul in the practice of Zen is an effective way to achieve such an illumination. By now the reader has some idea of how doing zazen and working on the *kikan* and *nantō* koans furnishes an effective way to accomplish emancipation from illusive tendencies. In short, as I said above, the reason that these tendencies are so ingrained is because the passions are so intimately linked to the flesh, and because the subconscious and karma also are closely bound up with the 'body'. Since in zazen a person's total mental and physical faculties are involved in this single act, which is accompanied by a great faith and a courage that reach to the deepest recesses of the 'body', the whole 'body' becomes awakened and enlightened. Therefore it should be unnecessary to explain further how effective zazen is in extending an enlightened eye throughout the 'body' so that 'the whole body is an eye'. At the same time, working on koans plays an important role in making the whole 'body' an eye, because when you put your whole 'body' into completely becoming the subject of the koan, it naturally resolves itself.

Becoming the subject of the koan means, as for example, in 'Great Master Ba is unwell' (*Hekigan-roku*, Case 3), that you yourself become Master Ba who is facing death. Unless you really die with your whole 'body', you will not be able to make an answer to this koan. But if you can become the dying Baso, it will be clear that you can die the Great Death, and from there a state of lofty wisdom and exalted and unrestricted activity will spring forth naturally. Isn't this the whole 'body' becoming more and more of an eye? To put it more explicitly, in zazen the mind and body are composed, all concepts are cut off, and the whole self is unified and concentrated. Then you break out of the shallow and narrow state of consciousness you had up to that moment and ascend to a higher and broader level of realization. There a land of greater freedom opens up, and your wisdom becomes loftier and broader in scope. At this point the koan solves itself; and with this your wisdom becomes conscious, clear, and unshakable. There is a Neoplatonic principle that says the higher the ability, the broader and deeper its power to extend and penetrate. Accordingly, this wisdom can be integrated into every crevice of the 'body' disciplining and ordering it. Then, at last, the whole body will be an eye which radiates the light of wisdom and lights up the world. I believe this is the thorough purification of the 'body' that is aimed at in Zen.

Chapter 5

What is true learning?

Hyakujō and the fox (*Mumonkan*, Case 2)

Eternal life (1 John 2)

Learning

I have learned many things from Zen, too many to enumerate. The first several chapters of this book were devoted to the main things Zen has taught me, and in this chapter I would like to relate one more.

But what does it mean to learn? Let us consider this question briefly before proceeding to the main subject. Generally we think that learning means to be taught something we did not know before by a teacher. This is called studying or acquisition of knowledge; the information or news considered so important by modern society is typical of it.

There is a more important aspect to learning, however. In the West it has been elucidated by Plato's theory of reminiscence. According to this theory, what we call learning is actually reminiscing. Plato believed that man's soul is immortal and harbours the seeds of all knowledge. In one sense, therefore, the soul knows the significance of everything. 'There is nothing to hinder a man, remembering only one thing (i.e., the one thing needed to remember is how to learn; also remembering is learning) — from himself finding out all else, if he is brave and does not weary in seeking' (Menon).

Learning in Zen basically resembles this theory of reminiscence. Zen teaches that all men are intrinsically Buddha and

that they need only to come to the realization of this fact;
hence, learning in Zen is to realize that you are intrinsically Buddha. In this respect it resembles Plato's theory, but
in another respect it is fundamentally different. In Plato's
theory it is a question of attaining knowledge by using the
intellect to recall it, whereas in Zen, one must die the Great
Death and be completely reborn. It is a becoming aware of
one's True Self for the first time through a conversion of the
whole person. The practical way of doing this kind of learning in Zen is mentally and physically to study the Way
through zazen.

The knowledge Zen has given me is not primarily academic.
The fundamental characteristic common to all the things I
have learned from Zen can be summed up as a realization of
my True Self through learning the Way with my whole self.

When I was studying theology, I was troubled by the lack
of balance between my intellectual knowledge and my
religious experience. Zen taught me how to solve this
problem. I would like to relate that experience here.

The Catholic theology I learned was, to put it simply, a
study of the 'events' related in the Bible. Its basis was the
'event' of God's revelation to us as recorded in Scripture.
What we call Catholic theology is a scholarly elucidation of
this 'event' according to Greek and modern thought. Since
Greek thought, especially Aristotelian philosophy, is intellectual and abstract, it is only natural for a theology that has
developed out of it also to be intellectual and abstract. As a
result, theology has drawn farther and farther away from the
'events' of the Bible, and because of that has tended to
become abstract opinion that is cut off from the living
Christian experience. This was the source of my difficulty.

An imbalance of scholarship and faith

Three years after graduating from college, I entered the
Society of Jesus. My two years of novitiate were devoted to
spiritual training, much the same as in the life of a Zen monk.
After that I studied philosophy for three years, taught in a
junior school for a year, and then did four years of theology.

There is no denying that during these long years of study, I tended to attach great importance to the intellect. My intellectual understanding of Christianity deepened greatly, but I made little progress on the level of religious experience. Furthermore, I was lax in putting my faith into actual practice in my daily life. As a result, the imbalance between my academic learning and my faith, and between my intellectual understanding and my religious experience, increased with the years.

Now, as you know, Zen does not engage in useless abstract discussion. Its basic tenet can be called pointing directly to the mind, seeing into one's nature, and becoming Buddha. But that does not mean that it degenerates into an experientialism that disregards universal principles of truth. When a disciple presents his understanding to the master in *dokusan* (a private interview), he must express the raw experience of his enlightenment without using abstract words. Yet, it must at the same time be an interpretation that stands securely on universal principles of truth. Take the koan 'Jōshū's Mu', for example:

> Once a monk came to Master Jōshū and said 'Buddhism teaches that all sentient beings have the Buddha-nature, but does a dog have it, too?' Jōshū answered, 'Mu' (no) (*Mumonkan*, Case 1).

This is such a famous koan that I think there is no necessity to explain it in detail. When working on this koan, a Zen practitioner does not reflect intellectually about the Buddhist teaching 'All sentient beings have the Buddha-nature'. Instead, he puts aside all reasoning and intellectual processes, sits upright, regulates his breathing, and recites 'Mu' with 'no-mind', becoming completely united with this Mu. Then, going back to his own Self, which is nothing other than the Buddha-nature, he awakens to his Primal Face. This Primal Face has a common source with all things. Therefore when a person awakens to his own Primal Face, he understands clearly the fundamental truth that all things are oneself, that the whole is the part. To put it more simply, it becomes evident that all creation is Buddha's life. Universal principles pulsate through this Zen experience, even though at this point they are not yet expressed abstractly.

You must first eliminate all intellectual speculation about what Mu is. Sit in the lotus position, regulate your breath, and simply and undistractedly recite 'Mu', becoming completely one with it. 'After a while when your efforts come to fruition, inside and out will become one naturally' (*Mumonkan*, Case 1). With this, you will awaken to your Original Self. It is simultaneously an awakening to the 'oneself' that has the same source as all creation. If we were to express it in abstract terms, we would say that all things are oneself, the whole is the part, the many are one, and so on. Such abstractions may not be used in the *dokusan* room, but the interpretations given there must have these theories as their backbone.

The theory of skiing

In the course of working on koans, I noticed a relation between universal principles and the *kenshō* experience, which I shall try to explain with an example from skiing. Someone who has theoretically learned how to ski from a book cannot really be said to have acquired the art of skiing. He has actually to slide down snow-covered slopes on skis and make the theory of skiing come alive in the act of skiing before he can become a good skier. Then it will no longer be merely an academic theory or an intellectually grasped abstraction, but something that is alive in his body. In this way, the real theory constitutes the act of skiing itself. Skiing that is not founded on firm theory is usually self-styled, poor and slow to progress. And, of course, a person who does such skiing is unable to teach others.

It is the same with a Zen *kenshō*. Even though you may learn Buddhist theory academically, it will not result in a Zen experience. But, at the same time, Zen does not ignore Buddhist theory; it experiences the universal principles of truth with mind and body. When a person has *kenshō*, these universal principles are alive in his mind and body and form a living framework for the enlightenment experience. Enlightenment is not viewing the universal principles as objects; rather, it is becoming aware of them in one's living self. Thus *kenshō* (literally, seeing into your nature) is not seeing your True Nature as an object; rather, the True Nature becomes the thing seeing. That is why a *kenshō* that does not stand on universal principles of truth is not the genuine article. And it goes without saying that such a religious experience cannot be a guide for others nor can it accomplish the Bodhisattva's task of saving all beings.

The koan 'Hyakujō and the fox'

I would like to go into the connection between *kenshō* and universal principles of truth a little more by examining the koan 'Hyakujō and the fox'.

> Whenever Master Hyakujō gave a sermon, an old man was always there listening with the monks, and leaving when they did. One day, however, he stayed behind, so the master asked him, 'Who are you, standing there in front of me?' The old man replied, 'I am not a human being. In the time of the Kashō Buddha, I was a Zen priest on this mountain. Once a monk asked me, "Does an enlightened person fall under the law of cause and effect or not?" I answered, "He does not fall under the law of cause and effect." For this, I fell to the state of a fox for five hundred lives. I implore you now, Master, to say a turning word on my behalf and release me from the body of a fox.' Then he asked, 'Does an enlightened person fall under the law of cause and effect or not?' The master answered, 'The law of cause and effect cannot be ignored.' When he heard this, the old man was immediately enlightened . . . [The remainder of the koan is omitted here] (*Mumonkan*, Case 2).

The Master Hyakujō in this koan is Ekai Zenji (720-814), who lived in Daichi Monastery on Mount Hyakujō. He was the first formally to draw up rules and regulations for Zen monasteries. Called Hyakujō's Pure Standards, they have been the model for Zen monastic rule to this day.

The Buddhist teaching on karma and emptiness (Sūñyata)

The law of cause and effect is one of the central teachings of Buddhist doctrine, and the present koan has a very interesting relation to this principle. Let us look at it first from the side of doctrine. Cause and effect is also called karma. All existence appears and disappears as a result of karma. Why? Because the true nature of all things is emptiness and their occurrence therefore depends on conditions and causes. All things come into being as a result of this karma and emptiness. Moreover, these two are simultaneously 'not the same and not separate' (*fusoku-furi*) and make up one reality. In this koan, the words 'He does not fall under the law of cause and effect' mean he has separated from cause and effect and is free; it therefore corresponds to emptiness.

'He does not ignore cause and effect' means he does not ignore the law but lives according to cause and effect; this corresponds to karma. Accordingly, if we consider karma and emptiness as 'not the same and not separate', thereby forming one reality, then not falling under cause and effect and not ignoring it are also 'not the same and not separate', and make up one reality. Doctrinally speaking, this is the universal principle that has to be grasped in this koan.

This kind of doctrinal explanation, however, is merely empty theory that is understood intellectually. The real law of cause and effect is a living law which provides the framework for all things. It is like the true theory of skiing that is alive in the person of the skier. How can one experience this living law? Thinking up answers to this question is useless. An excellent way to realize the law of cause and effect is to learn the Way of Zen with mind and body. It is just as in skiing where the only way to make progress is to bodily ski. You cannot understand the law of cause and effect until you cut off all theorizing and completely become the fox. Why? Because the law of cause and effect governs all things and is constantly constituting and keeping alive both you and the fox, so that when you completely become the fox, the law is realized in you and shows itself openly. At this, the words 'When the Zen practitioner becomes one with a koan, even without being sought for, *kenshō* comes forth of itself' are fulfilled.

The lack of refinement is also refinement

Now, what happens when a person realizes this law of cause and effect? Acting in accord with the law, which governs nature and the entire world, that person is able to live in perfect freedom. Master Tōin Iida explains it as follows:

> A fox that is content to live as a fox, without envying others, is called a Buddha. A man who is dissatisfied and looking for something else is called a fox. Look! When he freed himself from [the body of] the fox behind the rock, he didn't lose or gain even a hair. He cried when he was born and rotted when he died like everyone else. The lack of refinement is also refinement. Hyakujō conducted the funeral service for a dead monk. His action was praiseworthy indeed! He showed that when it comes to living at peace, it makes no difference to cause and effect whether one is a monk or a fox. A peaceful life is to forget yourself completely and be what you are.

We can see from this that the point of the koan is not just to apprehend the Buddhist doctrine of cause and effect intellectually, but to experience it bodily and be able to live a life of unrestricted activity. In accordance with the law of cause and effect, the weather is bad some days and fine on others. During the course of your life, there may be times when you will be sick or fail at something, but if at such times you cultivate 'no-mind' and become completely one with what you are engaged in doing, you will be able to live a full and rich life. I think this was the secret of the great men of Zen in all ages who lived a life of buoyant freedom like 'clouds blown by the wind and water flowing with the current'.

If Zen ignored universal principles and stressed experience only, the problem that I mentioned had been troubling me might never have been solved. If I had learned that kind of Zen, I probably would have ignored theology and let myself be carried away by Christian experience. This would have resulted in an even greater loss of spiritual balance. A state of spiritual balance is not achieved until both doctrine and experience are made alive and harmoniously united. True Zen breaks through the state of immobility brought on by stuffing one's head too full of doctrine; it creates a person in whom doctrine is operative in the sense explained above, and in whom both doctrine and experience are harmoniously integrated.

Through Zen, I was changed into a person who subjectively lives doctrine, and this existential change has extended into my life as a Christian. As a result, I have gradually changed from a man whose head was swollen out of proportion with theology into one who lives Christian teaching bodily. I did not purposely apply the methods I had learned from Zen to my Christian life. Rather, as I dedicated myself to the way of Zen, my life as a Christian gradually changed of itself. Catholic theology and Christian experience came to be united in my actual being, so that my problem disappeared of its own accord. I should mention here that I discovered my long, hard years of theological study had not been a waste. To a person who has never had the experience this may sound strange, but by practising Zen I not only learned about Buddhism, I also came to understand Christianity much better than before.

As the Spirit breathes

Let me try to explain this from the point of view of the real essence of Christianity, the 'event' of God's revelation. This revelation was gradually advanced through the course of Israelite history, finally reaching its zenith in the life of Christ. The 'events' of the life of Christ — his passion, death on the cross, and resurrection — are Self-revelations of Almighty God. Christ's preaching only explained the 'event' of this divine revelation in an incomplete form. His disciples bodily experienced this 'event' of Christ and saw the true life of God in it. St John summarizes this experience as follows:

> the life was made manifest, and we saw it, and testify to it, and proclaim to you the eternal life which was with the Father and was made manifest to us (1 John 1:2).

Moreover, this eternal life was given to the disciples, and they became conscious of the fact that they were living by it. 'The life was made manifest, and we saw it' does not only refer to seeing 'eternal life' in the life of Christ. It also means that they realized they were living the same life. Christ's life and our life are 'not the same and not separate'. We live the same life as Christ.

In addition, we can say that the real essence of Christianity is not in Christian doctrine, but in our common life with Christ. Doctrine is the principle which forms this life from the beginning. Christ preached it orally, the disciples developed it concretely, and in later generations theologians gave scholarly explanations of it in terms of Greek and modern thought. Thus an abstract system of theology came into being. The origin of this theological theory was the principle underlying the common life with Christ.

As a Christian, I am always living a Christian life. And yet what in Buddhism is called the True Self does not live separately from the Christian life in me. Therefore as I devote myself to the practice of Zen and awaken to my True Self, it is natural for me also to awaken to the Christian life with which it is one. If we consider it in this way, we can see it is not so strange that the practice of Zen should have led me to an understanding of true Christianity.

Now, what sort of state does the person who is able to awaken to this 'eternal life' attain to? If the man of Zen who gives witness to the law of cause and effect in himself attains a state of freedom, then, in a similar way, the Christian who realizes 'eternal life' will surely be filled with the Spirit of God and lead a truly happy life. A person who has awakened to the 'eternal life' sees clearly that the breath of that life is continually moving the whole world. He therefore lets that breath blow him as it pleases and lives a life of unparalleled freedom and delight.

Part II

Koans and the Bible

Chapter 6

Silence Speaks

Jesus and the adulterous woman (John 8:2-11)

The koan 'Gutei holds up a finger'
(*Mumonkan*, Case 3)

Before the woman taken in adultery

The following is one of my favourite passages in the Bible:

Early in the morning he came again to the temple; all the people
came to him, and he sat down and taught them. The scribes and the
Pharisees brought a woman who had been caught in adultery and
placing her in the midst they said to him, 'Teacher, this woman has
been caught in the act of adultery. Now in the law Moses commanded
us to stone such. What do you say about her?' This they said to test
him, that they might have some charge to bring against him. Jesus
bent down and wrote with his finger on the ground. And as they
continued to ask him, he stood up and said to them, 'Let him who is
without sin among you be the first to throw a stone at her.' And
once more he bent down and wrote with his finger on the ground.
But when they heard it, they went away, one by one, beginning with
the eldest, and Jesus was left alone with the woman standing before
him. Jesus looked up and said to her, 'Woman, where are they? Has
no one condemned you?' She said, 'No one, Lord.' And Jesus said,
'Neither do I condemn you; go, and do not sin again' (John 8:2-11).

A Zen monk I know told me he was deeply moved when
he read this passage. He added, 'Don't you think we can infer
from this incident in the Bible that Jesus had the same
experience that we have in Zen?'
Certainly a person who reads this passage with a silenced

heart will perceive that the Christ pictured there radiates a peace and lucidity that could be called Zen-like. Something about him resembles the ancient Zen masters who are described in the *Soshi-roku* (Records of the Patriarchs).

I would like to try to point out some of the similarities that can be found between this passage and the koan 'Gutei holds up a finger'. The first point of resemblance one notices is that both Christ and Gutei, when presented with a difficult problem that cannot be solved intellectually, are able to resolve it ingeniously. Second, in solving the problem, they both use unexpected actions or, rather, respond with silence. That is, they reply with an answer that is not an answer. Third, although replying in plain and simple language, they lead the questioner to self-introspection. Furthermore, their simple words produce greater results than the most exhaustive explanations could. In the fourth place, both of them transcend the dualistic opposition of whether or not to punish and, in going beyond punishment and non-punishment, take a stand of a higher dimension.

The problem put to Christ sprang from a desire to trap him. The Pharisees' questions are full of hostility. Catching a woman in adultery, they drag her before Christ where she presents a pitiful sight in her shame and disgrace. 'According to the teaching of love which you preach,' the Pharisees press Jesus, 'this woman must be forgiven. But to do so would go against the Law of Moses, which is the supreme law for us Jews. Moses commands that a woman who commits adultery should be stoned to death. By what authority do you break the law? But if you say that she should be stoned as Moses commands, you contradict your own teaching of love. Well, what do you say?'

Silence speaks

Several years ago, at the height of the campus unrest, I had the experience of being surrounded by ten or so left-wing students who made me the target of their vehement questioning. Carried away by the violent emotions characteristic of youth, the angry students showered me with cutting questions.

Every time I read this passage about the woman caught in adultery, the oppressive sensation I felt at that time comes back to me. Wasn't the situation Christ was placed in something like that? In such a case, the ordinary person is thrown off balance and cannot respond appropriately. But Jesus never lost his tranquillity. Not only that; by his silence he calmed the violent emotions of his opponents and exposed the hypocrisy of their argument.

Actually, it was only after I had begun to study Zen that I noticed this. I had understood before, in an intellectual way, that silence is speech and that more can be taught by it than by oral preaching, but it was only after I really began to do zazen that I learned it with my 'body'. And it is only recently that I have begun to become aware that man is intrinsically endowed with the power to teach, and even change, others without doing or saying a thing. The silent figure of my Zen master during *dokusan* has done a great deal to help me realize this, of course. This silent teaching in the *dokusan* room is an immediate communication of wisdom from mind to mind; inexpressible in words, it is therefore not something that can be explained here. A phenomenological account of the 'body language' mentioned above, however, may give us a clue to its explanation. Therefore, keeping what has been said thus far in mind, I would like to go more deeply into a Zen koan as an example of how we might approach the non-verbal 'language' of Jesus's 'body'.

The 'body' speaks

As is clear from the phenomenology of the 'body', the 'body' speaks without uttering a word. This 'body language' precedes oral language by its very nature and is, at the same time, the source of speech. Oral language is adapted to a topic of a particular time and place and is limited by these circumstances. Besides, speech cannot communicate everything. Rather, as we have all experienced frequently in everyday life, the more words used, the less their import. 'Body language', however, is the source of oral language and is like an inexhaustible fountain; it 'speaks' of the whole person in inexpressible 'words'.

Moreover, it is through the 'body' rather than through words that the thoughts at the bottom of one's heart emerge. The 'body language' described by Binswanger is a good example of this. Among the patients he was treating, there was a young woman who wanted desperately to see her sweetheart but was forbidden to do so by her mother. Incapable of venting her anger by attacking or rebelling against the mother, she lived each day in a state of discontent. One day, the young woman was seized by a sudden fit of belching, hiccupping and vomiting and became ill. An examination at a hospital for internal medicine revealed no physical cause for the sickness. She then consulted Dr Binswanger's department of psychiatry. Lengthy examinations finally showed that, unable to express her feelings of rebellion against her mother orally, the patient was speaking with her 'body'. Her belching and throwing-up were saying that she could not 'swallow' her mother's cruel prohibition and that she had to vomit it out. This is a pathological case, but the normal person too is incapable of expressing his innermost thoughts verbally; he must 'speak' them with his 'body'. And man's highest and most profound act, a religious experience, is even less amenable to verbal expression. It can only be transmitted by letting the whole 'body' speak.

Returning to 'Gutei holds up a finger'

I would like once more to ponder the koan 'Gutei holds up a Finger'. It is said that after his great enlightenment, Master Gutei never preached with words but always directed his disciples by simply holding up one finger. How was such a thing possible? According to the phenomenology of the 'body', it can be explained in the following way.

Gutei was a person who had attained the highest state of realization, a fact that must have been vividly manifested in his 'body'. But to perceive this lofty state through Gutei's 'body', the observer had to have a discerning eye. One who lacks such an eye cannot hear 'body language'. And when Gutei was sitting quietly, with his 'body' in repose, it must have been even more difficult to penetrate his state of realization. How then could an unenlightened disciple be helped to open his eye in order to hear this 'body language' and awaken to his Primal Face? The first way that comes to mind is oral preaching. Simple and obvious, it is the method ordinarily used in teaching religion. For leading a person to the deepest of religious experiences (the enlightenment of Zen or a Christian mystical experience), however, it is not only inadequate but could even be the cause of a false experience. There are two reasons for this. First of all, enlightenment is an existential conversion of the whole person and therefore cannot be brought about by oral persuasion.

Second, the state of enlightenment cannot be explained in words. If one tries to give a verbal explanation of it, he ends up with a rice cake painted on paper, i.e. it looks like, but is totally different from, the real thing. The more words used in an explanation, the more the listener pursues the meanings associated with them and the further he draws away from the path to enlightenment.

In order to lead his disciples to enlightenment, therefore, Gutei devised the unique method of sticking up a finger. This unexpected gesture startled the disciple and forced him to abandon his previous habit of thinking only in terms of meaning. By throwing his whole person into this seemingly senseless gesture of holding up a finger, Gutei thrust it before the other as something full of meaning, so that the disciple was naturally taken aback by it. The significant world he had held up to that time was toppled and rendered completely meaningless by the 'senseless', that is to say totally significant, holding up of a finger. This was the raised finger functioning as a killing sword. But it simultaneously had the activity of a life-giving sword. By holding up his finger with all the energy of his body and soul, Gutei perfectly manifested his True Self. Therefore his 'body' was filled with vigour and exerted force upon the disciple, bringing him to an existential conversion and, at the same time, awakening him to his True Self. It goes without saying that at this moment an overflowing of vitality equivalent to Gutei's hurtling power was necessary on the part of the disciple.

The 'speech' of the silent Jesus

If this speech of Gutei's lifted finger is applied to the 'body language' of the silent Christ, we will be able to understand the deeper content of the Scriptural passage. When the adulterous woman is brought before Jesus and he is pressed to answer the Pharisees' question, he keeps silent, but this seeming gesture of defeat is 'speaking' with great power. The crowd around Jesus probably expected him to give an eloquent reply. Instead, he surprises them by remaining silent. As was true in the case of Gutei's holding up a finger, he shocks them by doing something unexpected and makes them doubt their customary way of thinking.

Christianity teaches that Christ undertook death on the cross because of his ardent desire to save mankind. Concentrating the energy of his whole body and mind into this ardent desire, which permeated his entire existence, he keeps silent. If this is so, then the 'body' of Christ must be speaking of his unfailing wish to save all men. This aspiration is not extinguished by his keeping silent. If he had attempted instead to explain this immeasurable and inexpressible desire, its real meaning would have been lost on the crowd. Conversely, by keeping silent the 'speech' of his whole 'body' emerges and the unfailing desire is manifest to all. Silence may appear meaningless, but, in fact, it is replete with meaning. By this 'meaningless meaning', the conventional mentality of the crowd and the Pharisees (that in accordance with the Law of Moses an adulterous woman should be stoned to death) is put in question and rendered meaningless. This is the activity of Christ's killing sword of silence. Was it not because the Pharisees were struck by this sword that they felt uneasy about persisting with their questioning? Jesus then said, 'Let him who is without sin among you be the first to throw a stone at her,' and was again silent. This forced the Pharisees to examine their own consciences and they could no longer remain before him.

It can be said further that the silent 'body' of Christ is also a life-giving sword. That is because it proclaims his earnest desire for the salvation of mankind and 'speaks' of the infinite love with which he died on the cross. What should one do to become able to hear this 'speaking'? Just as Gutei's followers had to become one with him by dying the Great Death in order to hear what his uplifted finger was saying, so those who wish to hear the infinite love that Christ's 'body' is 'speaking' must be ready to be crucified with him and die the Great Death in the Christian sense of the words.

Chapter 7

A thrust home

Cross-examination on the koan 'Mu'

A camel and the eye of a needle (Mark 10:25)

A camel and the eye of a needle

There are many Biblical passages that are extremely obscure. Some of them might even be called incomprehensible paradoxes. Take the following passage for example:

> It is easier for a camel to go through the eye of a needle than for a rich man to enter the kingdom of heaven (Mark 10:25).

This is generally interpreted as a metaphor used by Jesus to explain how difficult it is to enter heaven. To be sure, it is a metaphor, but most interpretations fail to see the contradiction contained in it and as a result they circumvent the cutting edge of the existential question it poses. In fact, this passage is a difficult and paradoxical problem. It is an existential question directed to each one of us, and in it is hidden a blade to gouge out our attachments. If we overlook this we will not be able to understand why the disciples were so astonished at hearing these words, and we will end up unable to grasp their real meaning.

Shortly after I started to practise Zen, I was given the chance to realize the true significance of this passage. But in order to tell about this experience, it is necessary to explain the particulars of Zen practice. The first problem that is ordinarily presented to the beginner in Zen is either the koan 'Mu' or 'The Sound of One Hand'. The latter was devised by

Hakuin Zenji for the training of his disciples and is the following sort of seeming contradiction. If you clap both hands together it will produce a sound, but one hand alone makes no sound. 'Hear the sound of one hand.' This is the problem conceived by Hakuin.

The Zen student has to solve this paradox, but no amount of mulling it over in his mind will produce a solution. Then what should he do? There is only one way for the practitioner to solve this problem: he must make a fundamental change in his habitual way of thinking. When he goes to *dokusan* he is given guidance by the master, but it basically comes down to direction in a single method. And that method is to get rid of his own thinking and attain the same state of consciousness as Hakuin, who devised the koan, so that he can see things with the same eye Hakuin did. In the case of the koan 'Mu' the situation is identical: the student must have the same eye as Master Jōshū who appears in the koan. Mumon describes this state very accurately:

> Not only will you see Jōshū face to face, but you will also walk hand in hand with the whole descending line of Zen masters and be eyebrow to eyebrow with them. You will see with the same eye they see with and hear with the same ear (*Mumonkan*, Case 1).

This penetrating 'eye' is not obtained until you reach a state of transcendence. The reason 'The Sound of One Hand' seems contradictory to a person is not because he is mentally incompetent or slow, but because, under the sway of selfishness and egoism, he is living a life of attachment. But if a person cuts off all attachments and attains a state of freedom, he will develop a 'discerning eye'.

Putting yourself in the place of the other

At first glance, this kind of Zen experience seems to be very remote from the life of the ordinary person, but it is not really. Everyone has probably has the following experience at some time. You are having an argument with someone and just cannot see the other person's point of view. Later, however, when you have calmed down and your own ego has disappeared, you can fully appreciate the other's position, even though it was so hard to see at the height of the quarrel. The Zen experience mentioned above is nothing but a deepening of this experience. But you must be able to put yourself in the other's place immediately, at any time and under any circumstances, whether the other is your opponent in a dispute, an animal, a plant or even an inanimate object. It will not do to put yourself in the other's place *after* the quarrel. You must do it instantly and directly. Then you will be able to hear the sound of one hand for yourself. In this case, the 'other' is one hand. When you become the one hand, you will naturally hear the sound of its voice without even trying, because you and the hand are not two separate things.

Now, after the practitioner has passed this koan, the master bombards him with some twenty or thirty cross-examining questions to determine whether he has really understood it or not. At the same time, he is polishing the disciple's eye so that he may see even better. An example of such a cross-examining question is 'Pass through the stem of a tobacco pipe'; or another: 'If you were locked in a stone chest, how would you get out?' Such questions are paradoxical puzzles to the ordinary person, but for one who has passed 'Mu' or 'The Sound of One Hand', and attained a 'discerning eye', they are not difficult.

When I was able to see into several such problems, the Biblical passage quoted above suddenly flashed across my mind. For a long time, I had been unable to resolve the paradox in this passage, but the moment I could solve the Zen questions, I was able to realize its deeper meaning. Later, when I looked up its context, I was surprised to see how similar it was to that of the examination by the master. But first, let us refer again to the context of the latter.

The 'context' of cross-examining questions

The context of cross-examining questions is not expressed verbally. Rather, the 'context' in each case is the state of affairs before and after the master asks these questions of the disciple. Through arduous practice, the latter gets rid of his egotistic attachments and finally leaping into a new land of freedom, opens his enlightened eye. This moment is the true centre of the 'context'. The master does not pass up the opportunity presented by this maturing of the disciple's state of realization. With lightning speed, he starts to cross-examine the disciple, pressing him for answers. Presented with these puzzles, the disciple is surprised at first, and at a loss for an answer. But if he immediately returns to his enlightenment experience and deepens it, he becomes able to see in an absolutely new way by putting himself in the place of all other things and the answer comes forth of itself.

What about the context of the Scriptural passage quoted above? On the whole, it is expressed in the sentences there, but we should not overlook the important 'context' that is concealed in the existential attitude of the persons who are speaking. To begin with, let us pursue the context contained in the sentences and then look, when necessary, at the 'context' concealed in the people who are talking together. A certain man asked Jesus, 'What must I do to inherit eternal life?' Jesus expounded the main admonitions of the Ten Commandments. The man said, 'All these I have observed from my youth.' Perceiving the man's sincerity and fidelity in this answer, Jesus went one step further:

> And Jesus looking upon him loved him, and said to him, 'You lack one thing; go, sell what you have, and give to the poor, and come, follow me.' At that saying his countenance fell, and he went away sorrowful; for he had great possessions.
>
> And Jesus looked around and said to his disciples, 'How hard it will be for those who have riches to enter the kingdom of God!' And the disciples were amazed at his words. But Jesus said to them again, 'Children, how hard it is to enter the kingdom of God! It is easier for a camel to go through the eye of a needle than for a rich man to enter the kingdom of God.' And they were exceedingly astonished, and said to him, 'Then who can be saved?' Jesus looked at them and said, 'With men it is impossible, but not with God; for all things are possible with God' (Mark 10:21-27).

Jesus looked at them

There are many things in this passage that need explaining
from the exegetic standpoint, but I should like to indicate
only the most important points of the problem that confronts
us. In two places it says that Jesus looked at someone and
that his words at those times were filled with deep feeling. In
the first instance, the Gospel adds that he 'loved (*agapaō*)
him'. *Agapaō* means to care greatly for someone, as well as to
have respect for the other's personality which is revealed
positively through the conduct of your whole person. This
must have been shown by Jesus's attitude, but we should also
read his affection in his words that followed. On the surface
they are the severe demand to give up everything and become
a follower of Christ and pose a difficult challenge. But the
truth is that these words are a compassionate blessing. The
rich man could not realize that, however. Why not? Because
'he had great possessions.' As long as he was attached to his
wealth, Jesus's words appeared to be unreasonable demands,
and he could not grasp their real meaning. This is similar to
the case of the first Zen koans which I mentioned earlier. To
a person encapsulated in selfishness, the koan 'The sound of
one hand' seems like a paradoxical riddle. But when such a
person is stripped of attachment and becomes a free body
through the practice of Zen, he can solve it easily.

What about the disciples? In the sentence immediately
following the above quotation, Peter says that they have
responded to this stringent demand by gladly giving up
everything to follow him, and Jesus acknowledges this
(Mark 10:28).

A thrust home

We should notice that from the contextual standpoint, the
difficult problem of the camel and the eye of a needle is
directed, not to the rich man, but to the disciples. In other
words, Jesus is not preaching to those who do not follow
him; instead he is challenging the disciples who have left all
to follow him. Jesus appears to be perplexing the disciples

by making unreasonable demands, but it is hardly necessary to explain that, in truth, this is a loving act of kindness on his part. This oral exchange is not dissimilar to the cross-examination a master gives a disciple who has just passed the first barrier in Zen.

Seeing that his disciples are surprised, Jesus bewilders them further by speaking even more enigmatically, and their astonishment increases. In the Japanese translation of this passage it is recorded twice that the disciples were 'astonished'. In the Greek original, however, two different words are used. When the disciples were 'astonished' at Jesus's words 'How hard it will be for those who have riches to enter the kingdom of God', the passive form of the verb *Thambéō*, meaning to be surprised and frightened, is used. But when they are 'astonished' at Christ's words 'It is easier for a camel to go through the eye of a needle than for a rich man to enter the kingdom of God', the Greek original is *Perissoos eksepléssonto*. This does not simply mean to be surprised; it has the more intense meaning of being thunderstruck and frightened out of one's wits. Why did Jesus do such a thing to the disciples? Why was it an act of kindness for him to put them in a dilemma, confuse them, and then alarm them even more? There can only have been one reason: it was necessary for the education of the disciples and without it their imperfections would not have been corrected.

Why were the disciples astounded?

Actually, the disciples' astonishment was due not only to the incomprehensibility of Christ's words, but also to their own state of imperfection. That is to say, the reason they failed to understand was not because they were illiterate or stupid, but because they still had faults and attachments in their hearts. They had responded to Jesus's demand by giving up everything to follow him, so there was a marked difference between them and the rich man who 'went away sorrowful'. It was the decisive difference of being or not being a disciple of Jesus. They had put their complete trust in him. Being disciples meant that they had put their lives and fate into his hands and would live and die with Jesus. But among the disciples there were various levels of men and differences in their depth. To be sure they were men who had 'left everything' (Mark 10:28), but they were still imperfect. This is clear from the fact that immediately afterwards, when Jesus prophesied his passion, not only were they unable to realize what he was saying, but they were even looking to their own glory and started an ugly argument about it among themselves.

The subjective reason for the disciples' astonishment should be evident from the above, but what about the objective reason for their surprise? Scripture scholars say the Jews of that time thought that wealth was a sign of God's favour, and we should bear this fact in mind. But that was not the real object of their surprise. Rather, they were astonished to hear that unless a rich man gave up all his possessions, he would not be able to enter the kingdom of God. In other words, they thought that the demand that a rich man renounce all his wealth was too harsh, if not impossible. But the disciples understood that Jesus was not directing the words about the camel going through the eye of a needle to the rich man alone, for they all said in unison, 'Then who can be saved?' If Jesus had been referring only to rich people, it would not have concerned them and they would not have been so thunderstruck. It was because they knew his words were directed to them that they felt so threatened. They must have been so astonished and frightened because they interpreted these words to mean that it would be easier for a camel to go through the eye of a needle than for themselves to enter the kingdom of God. The disciples had given up everything to follow Christ, but I think they were worried about whether they could continue to meet his stringent requirements for entering the kingdom of God. If we look at it this way, we can also understand the sentence that followed: 'Jesus looked at them and said, "With men it is impossible, but not with God; for all things are possible with God." '

Killing and giving life

As I said before, we can see Jesus's deep feeling in the words
'Jesus looked at them'. He was about to say something of
extreme personal importance to the disciples. Hence, we
cannot construe that he was just teaching a general doctrine
regarding man's incompetence and God's omnipotence. Such
an interpretation would completely disregard the context.
Jesus is teaching the amazed disciples something gravely
important from the bottom of his heart. As I mentioned
above, he had seen through the disciple's imperfections,
which were the underlying cause of their amazement. He
threatened them, made them feel uneasy, then completely
stunned them, and intended to deal the final blow with these
words. Now, in what did the disciples' imperfection lie? If we
conjecture inversely from what Jesus said, it appears the
disciples were pessimistic about their ability to make the
complete abandonment required to enter the kingdom of
God. Didn't they unconsciously believe that their giving up
everything to follow Jesus had been accomplished through
their own human power? I think this idea was hidden deep
in the disciples' unconscious. It caused them to be proud
and implicitly attribute all their good deeds to their own
virtue, and to make their following of Jesus a means to their
own 'glory'. Even though right after this Jesus prophesied
his passion, two of the disciples begged to be included in
Christ's glory, and when the others heard of it they became
resentful. This incident shows us there was still a deep
attachment to self embedded in their hearts. If they still had
these feelings, it was only natural that they could not understand Jesus's words about the camel passing through the eye
of a needle and that they were so astonished by them.

If we regard the above conjecture as correct, then the
reason Jesus said those words looking them in the face was to
kill their hidden attachments and make them alive with the
divine life. This can truly be called 'a thrust home'. In other
words, Jesus is not teaching doctrine, but is forcing the
disciples to make an existential conversion. What Jesus
desired most ardently was that they die to themselves and
live in God. With these words he wanted to kill the disciples

and bring them back to life.

If, as Jesus wished, the disciples had been able to make a real conversion of self, the words about a camel passing through the eye of a needle would not have seemed paradoxical or thrown them into such consternation. If they had been able to let go of all attachment to thoughts of 'Me, me!' and put themselves in the other's place, so that they could view everything from the side of God, the fact that 'all things are possible with God' would have been a clear and shining reality for them. There would have been no room for anxiety or astonishment. Their whole being would have overflowed with unrestricted creativity and the confidence that by the power of God they could easily pass through this reality, which is more difficult than a camel going through the eye of a needle.

Thus far, I have been pointing out how Zen koans and cross-examining questions resemble this Biblical passage, and I would like to carry this comparison through to one last level. In most cases, when cross-examined by the master and confronted with a difficult problem, a Zen disciple is also perplexed and sometimes even struck dumb with astonishment. But he must remain undaunted by this and work to get rid of all egoism in order to deepen his enlightenment. The important thing at such a juncture is to return to the True Self. If a person does so, he will be able to put himself in the place of the other and develop a 'discerning eye' which sees everything from an absolutely new dimension. When the solution to a koan takes form in his mind, the disciple presents it to the master in *dokusan*. If the solution is correct, he is given the next koan to work on; if not, he is made to do it over again. If he has repeated the same koan many times and come to an impasse, the master will wait for the right moment and then, looking hard at the disciple, make a pertinent comment. Usually such comments are very short, a 'thrust home' to get the disciple out of the impasse. If the disciple's eye is opened by this thrust and his entire being converted so that he is completely transformed into someone who sees things from the other's point of view, the problem solves itself.

Chapter 8

When a single flower blooms it's spring everywhere

Jōshū's 'All things come back to one'
(*Hekigan-roku*, 45)

The sin of one man and the death of all men
(Romans 5:12-19)

The dynamic dialectic of the part and the whole

Among the most difficult passages in the Bible is the following one by St Paul:

> For as by a man came death, by a man has come also the resurrection of the dead. For as in Adam all die, so also in Christ shall all be made alive (1 Corinthians 15:21-22).

In this passage, St Paul deliberately emphasizes the analogy of one man and all men. This is no mere rhetorical device, but an accurate expression of what he really wants to say. Paul is very fond of this idea and its expression. In Romans 5 he spends from verses 12 to 19 explaining it as follows:

> Therefore as sin came into the world through one man and death through sin, and so death spread to all men . . . . For if many died through one man's trespass, much more have the grace of God and the free gift in the grace of that one man Jesus Christ abounded for many . . . . Then as one man's trespass led to condemnation for all men, so one man's act of righteousness leads to acquittal and life for all men. For as by one man's disobedience many were made sinners, so by one man's obedience many will be made righteous.

Traditionally this has been a much-debated passage. In modern Scripture studies as well, the structure of Romans 5 has been the subject of exegetic controversy from the standpoint of content. The section from verse 12 to verse 21 in particular has been a point of dispute over the centuries because in comparing Christ's death on the cross to the sin of Adam, Paul sets forth an idea that has come to be of decisive importance in the history of Christian dogma. One reason it has caused so much controversy is because these sentences overflow with paradox. Why does the sin of one man extend to all men? Why by one man's disobedience do all men become sinners? Why does the resurrection of one man restore life to all? And why through the obedience of one do all become righteous?

Theological knowledge veils the eyes

Because we have studied some theology, we Christians take it for granted that Christ's grace is universal and extends to all men. We have learned that the single sin of Adam affects all mankind and have thereby become incapable of astonishment at the enormity of the universal effect of that sin. When we read the passage quoted above, aren't those of us who have this kind of theological understanding satisfied to take it simply as a confirmation of a doctrine we believe in? We accordingly overlook the essential contradiction contained in Paul's words and are insensitive to their latent power to shock. Theological knowledge is such a part of us that we are unable to fathom the deeper meaning of the Bible. Actually, when we read these words of Paul with an open mind, we ought to be surprised at the puzzling inconsistencies and paradoxes contained in them. We should be bewildered by the near incomprehensibility of their contents. It is odd if, on reading them, we do not feel any surprise or bewilderment, for what Paul is talking about here is the mystery of Christ's salvation and the mystery of Adam's iniquity (*mysterium iniquitatis*). Isn't it natural for a person to be amazed and nonplussed when confronted with a true mystery?

Now the contradictory dialectic of the one and the many, one person and all people, is not just the thought of Paul.

Jesus himself expresses the same idea in the Gospel in words that are slightly easier to understand. For example:

> Unless a grain of wheat falls into the earth and dies, it remains alone; but if it dies, it bears much fruit (John 12:24).

> And I, when I am lifted up from the earth, will draw all men to myself (John 12:32).

This dynamic relation between the one and the many, the contradictory dialectic of the part and the whole, is the central thought of Christian teaching. Yet Christian theology has not yet discovered a way to grasp this contradictory relation. I think this is true, in fact, not only of Christian theology, but of the whole of European thought. The Hegelian dialectic, for example, is a dialectic of the developmental process of thesis-antithesis-synthesis and cannot explain the circumstances by which the sin of one man at once becomes the sin of all mankind. Kierkegaard tried to explain it by means of a paradox, but the attempt could hardly be called successful.

As I came to deliberate on various Zen koans, I was surprised and delighted to discover that one of the central themes of the Zen experience was a dynamic grasp of the contradictory dialectic of the part and the whole, and the whole and the part. I realized that the Zen way of apprehending it could shed great light on the understanding of the puzzling Biblical passages quoted above. For that reason, I would like to tell about the Zen experience of the part and the whole.

Jōshū's curious reply

In the forty-fifth case of the *Hekigan-roku* there is a famous koan entitled 'Jōshū's all things come back to one'. When I passed this koan, I was able to realize the deep meaning of the above-mentioned words of the Bible. The koan goes as follows:

> A monk asked Jōshū, 'All things come back to one. Where does the one return to?' Jōshū said, 'When I was in the province of Sei, I made a robe. It weighed seven *kin*.'

The Jōshū in this koan is Jūshin Zenji (778-897), who lived in Jōshū Kannon Temple. The words and deeds of this master have been collected in the *Jōshū-roku* (The Jōshū Records) and show him to have been one of the greatest Zen masters of all time. A monk once asked him, 'All things ultimately come back to the original one. Then, where does this one return to?'

This is a very difficult question. The original one is called Buddha in Buddhism, or Mu or your Primal Face (True Self) in Zen. It probably corresponds to what is God for us Christians. All being ultimately comes back to this one. This is a fundamental teaching of Buddhism. But the question is, where does this one go? This is a grave problem.

To put it in theoretical terms, what does 'all is one and one is all' mean? More concretely, what does it mean to say that one drop of water, just as it is, is the whole ocean, and that conversely, the whole ocean, just as it is, is one drop of water? There is no point in trying to reason out an answer to this question for it contains a contradiction. It is usual to reflect logically that if all things come to one, then the one returns to all things. Anyone can make this kind of theoretical deduction, but that is not what is being asked here. The question is whether or not you can assent to the statement that all being, as it is, is an appearance of the one itself.

To this difficult question Jōshū replies calmly, 'When I was in my home town (Santō-shō) in Sei Province, I made a long hemp robe. It weighed some seven *kin* [about 2.5 kilograms].' To the person who is not practising Zen, these words are a complete enigma and it is difficult to see how they could be an answer to the monk's question. Therefore I would like to search out the real meaning of this koan while examining, at the same time, the process of Zen practice. It goes without saying that this process also has profound significance in regard to the understanding of the Biblical passages quoted above.

In my case, I was given this koan shortly after I had passed the first one and looked at two or three others. The purpose of this koan is to keep the practitioner, who has obtained a deep insight into 'Mu' (or his Primal Face) by passing a number of koans, from getting caught up in that

Mu and settling down in the world of non-discrimination.

The realization of Mu first comes when the Zen student has cut off all egotistic attachment and died the Great Death. It is to certify for oneself that 'all things have the same source'. It is the same as saying that one realizes that all being is kept alive by eternal life and that all things are equal. My self is not separate from the self of another person; I and the pen I am using, I and the cherry tree in the garden are not separate things. To put it more concretely, when talking to someone or doing a job with another person, I talk or work standing directly in the other's place, becoming one body with the other. When I write, I am one with the pen; and when I gaze at a cherry tree in the garden, I do it becoming the cherry tree itself. This is the experience of Mu. Needless to say, in order to do this I must die myself and become completely concentrated in a state of *samādhi*. But if a Zen practitioner should abide in this experience of 'non-discrimination' and settle down in it permanently, he has been led astray by *satori*. Such a person is admonished, 'Do not cling to the one either.' The koan 'All things come back to one' is a problem put to someone who is in just this kind of state.

Bringing everything to life

Now, what is it that the Zen student has to see clearly in this koan? Abstractly speaking, he must see distinction in equality. He has to realize that while all things are separate from each other, they are the appearances of oneness itself. To put it more concretely, when you are working with someone, for example, you will not be able to do a really good job if you see only the aspect of yourself and the other person being one body. You have to see the other's individuality and discern that that irreplacable other person, as he is in himself, is the True Self, before you can become one mind and body with him and bring to life the individuality of you both.

Master Sōgen Ōmori expresses this in more Zen-like language:

If we make all things coming back to one, the negative side, the dying the Great Death, then how about if we call the one coming back to all things the affirmative actualization of the Great Life? In all things coming back to one, there is the holding on whereby even real gold loses its colour; and in the one coming back to all things, there is the affirmative meaning of letting go whereby even tiles and pebbles sparkle (*Hekigan-roku Shiken* [Thoughts on the Blue Cliff Record], Hakujusha, Tokyo, 1976, II, pp.345-7).

Actually, Jōshū's seemingly irrelevant reply is an expression of his free and creative state in which the Great Life has been actualized. We must not overlook this. Breaking free of the experience of undifferentiated equality and leaping into the real world of differentiation, affirming all things, making use of all things with perfect freedom — this is the state of realization the practitioner must achieve through this koan. Master Ōmori describes this state of mind superbly:

With his reply, the sharp old veteran Jōshū topples the charging monk, who had been so determined to beat him with his question. With a flick of his hand he tosses him into the middle of the Western Lake. When this fellow, who was so burdened down with the troublesome baggage of 'the one', 'all things', and useless 'satori', had been dumped in the lake and let go of his burden, he felt light in mind and body and heaved a deep sigh of relief (*Ibid.*, p.347).

When a single flower blooms, it's spring everywhere

From olden times, the following Zen phrase has been appended to this koan: 'One speck of plum blossom and the three thousand worlds are fragrant.' While expressing Jōshū's state of realization, this verse, at the same time, gives a true picture of the world we live in. There are many other similar expressions in Zen: 'One speck of dust contains everything in the universe; one thought is endowed with the three thousand worlds': 'When a single flower blooms, it's spring everywhere.' These verses express the world seen by the person who has really passed the koan 'All things come back to the one'. When a person dies the Great Death and becomes a single plum blossom, he arrives at the origin of both the flower and himself. Then putting himself in the position that all is one and one is all, he is able to see clearly that the three thousand worlds are filled with the fragrance of that one blossom.

This kind of Zen experience may seem foreign to Christianity, but in fact it is not. A Christian friend once said to me, 'When you love someone with your whole heart and soul, by that act you simultaneously love all the people of the world.' These words express a deep experience founded on Christian faith. Any Christian who has had a deep spiritual experience will not find them difficult to understand. If such a person can transfer this experience from people to things, he may be able to infer somehow the state of realization aimed at in the koan 'All things come back to one'.

Now then, how does this Zen experience throw light on the interpretation of the passages from Scripture quoted earlier? First, it teaches us that the dynamic dialectical relationship between the part and the whole cannot be grasped by rational speculation. Instead we must abandon our egos and unite with God who is the Source of all creation. If we are able to become one with God through complete abandonment of self, it will be easy to see that all being is one in God. As a consequence, we shall be able to catch a glimpse into the mystery of how the God become man, Jesus Christ, made all men righteous by his death on the cross and rose again from the dead.

This alone, however, still will not give us an understanding of the relationship between Adam's sin and all mankind that Paul speaks of. Explaining the relation between Christ's death and the salvation of mankind by means of it only leaves it shrouded in a veil of obscurity. Limited as my knowledge is, I have yet to encounter a Scripture scholar who interprets these two points correctly or a student of dogma who explains them theologically.

The cross of Jesus and the resurrection of all men

The latter half of the koan 'All things come back to one', that is, the process of experiencing that 'The one comes back to all things', has great significance here. What I learned from 'The one comes back to all things' is that one must not rest on one's laurels in the *satori* of blind equality, but break free of it and come out into the real world of differentiation, making everything come alive by bringing out its full potential. In the same way, in the Christian experience one must not be completely immersed in the contemplative life of union with God but find God in all things of the real world and carefully make the most effective use of each one. More concretely, as my Christian friend said above, it is to love a fellow human being with your whole body and soul and to put your whole body and soul into examining any offence committed against another person. If you love someone with your whole body and soul, you should be able to see God and all mankind in that person. Likewise, if you thoroughly examine a grave sin that you have committed against another, you will realize what an infinite affront it is to God and what an act of faithlessness it is towards all men.

If we read Paul's words again with this spiritual insight, we ought to be able to understand what he is trying to say. First, a person who has thoroughly examined his sins will see how the one sin of Adam, head of the human race, could bring the horrendous destructive forces called Sin and Death to all mankind. And when a person with this insight loves a fellow human being with his whole body and soul, he is bound to realize how, as man, Jesus of Nazareth, by the single act of love called the crucifixion, could bring about the justification and resurrection of the human race. Furthermore, I believe that Paul infers the universal force of Christ's death from the effect of Adam's sin for the following reasons.

For us humans, the fact that we are sinners comes before the fact of our loving a fellow man, both in terms of time and of our real nature. Consequently, we are already aware of the fact of our sinfulness before we love someone with our whole body and soul, and this fact is more familiar to us. Therefore, by means of a thorough investigation of our sins, we feel the universal destructive force of Adam's sin before we become aware of the universal saving power of Christ's act of love by loving a fellow man, and it is more familiar to us. I think that if we reflect on it this way, we will be able to understand why Paul inferred the act of Christ's love from Adam's sin.

Chapter 9

No-mind and the mind of a child (1)

The koan 'Mu'

Admirable Records of Unmoving Wisdom

Bankei's Dharma Talks

'A baby's mind is Mu'

It is often said that what is called Mu or No-mind in Zen is
the same thing that Christ was speaking of when he said that
we must become like children. For example, Master Mumon
Yamada relates the following incident:

Once an American Catholic priest came to see me. He sat down in
front of me and said, 'Teach me the satori of Zen. Tell me what
state of mind a person attains when he is enlightened.' He was
certainly asking a lot! If the answer to that question could be put
into words and we could understand enlightenment just by hearing
about it, we wouldn't have to go to all this trouble doing zazen. The
priest probably thought that as long as he was in Japan, he'd have an
instant enlightenment before going home. I replied by saying,
'Before I answer your question, I've got one of my own. Christ said
that unless you have the mind of a little child you cannot enter
heaven. Now just what is the mind of a little child? What is the
psychological state of a baby? Someday you'll be going to heaven,
won't you? In what frame of mind do you intend to go?' The priest
became lost in deep thought. After a while, though, he came up with
a very fine answer, 'The mind of a baby is Mu.' He said the same
thing that Zen teaches. So I said, 'That's right. It's Mu and to understand what Mu is, is to be enlightened.' . . . Delighted, he slapped his
thigh and said, 'I understand!' 'It's too soon to feel so happy. You've
understood here [pointing to his head], but in Zen you have to

71

understand here [pointing to his *hara* or belly].' 'I majored in philosophy in college. If I understand up here, that's good enough' (*Mumon Hōwa-shū* [Mumon's Dharma Talks], Shunjūsha, Tokyo, 1972, p.45).

One hears the same sort of thing from the mouths of many Zen masters, but what does Christianity say about this? Various people have asked me. Therefore I would like to comment on this problem in some detail. Although I say 'comment on', I do not propose to attempt an abstract comparison of the two based on the pertinent literature and Scripture studies. That sort of abstract discussion will never bring us in touch with the core of the religious problem. Rather, presupposing this kind of knowledge, I would like to tackle the problem of the real essence of the Zen Mu and the childlikeness that Christ speaks about by meditating on it, deepening, at the same time, my own experience.

Now, everyone feels that he understands in some way what is meant by Mu in Zen and what Christ was talking about when he said we must become like children. But, at the same time, there is nothing more subtle and evasive. They share the common factor of being something we feel we understand somehow but really do not. Both are extremely simple, so that in one respect they can be grasped by anyone, but in another respect there is nothing that is more profound or incomprehensible. Therefore we should not conclude too easily that they are the same or be premature about deciding that they are absolutely different. Furthermore, neither can be completely realized by only one or two religious experiences. To understand them with the *hara* and then make that realization a part of yourself, putting it into practice in daily life, is the great work of a lifetime. Therefore what I am going to say below must be called a tentative answer made from my limited level of realization.

Understanding with the head and understanding with the hara

The above quotation from Master Mumon Yamada emphasizes the difference between understanding with the head and understanding with the *hara* or viscera. We have to make a strict distinction between these two ways of understanding in the case of both No-mind and childlikeness. Let us take this as the starting point of our consideration of them.

Mu is the first barrier of the Zen experience. Once a practitioner has met the master and made formal obeisance to him as a sign that he has become his disciple, he is usually given the koan 'Mu'. This was also true in my case. As was already mentioned, the koan 'Jōshū's dog' was the first problem that Master Ekai Mumon assigned his disciples to work on. He says in his commentary on this koan, 'In studying Zen, one must pass the barrier set up by ancient Zen masters.'

> A monk earnestly asked Master Jōshū, 'Does a dog have Buddha-nature?' Jōshū answered, 'Mu [No] !' (*Mumonkan*, Case 1).

Buddhism teaches that all beings have the Buddha-nature. A dog is no exception. But even though doctrinally speaking a dog has the Buddha-nature, on the level of common knowledge or practical experience we do not think that this is true. Perhaps the monk thrust this question at Jōshū because he was caught in a dilemma between Buddhist doctrine and practical wisdom. Jōshū simply answered, 'Mu!' What does this mean? 'Mu' can be translated as 'no' or 'nothing', but Jōshū is not saying that there is no Buddha-nature in a dog. If he were, it would be a contradiction of Buddhist teaching, and one of the most eminent masters in Zen history would hardly be denying a fundamental tenet of Buddhism. When he was asked the identical question on another occasion, moreover, the same Jōshū answered, 'U [Yes]!' We can infer, therefore, that this 'Mu' transcends yes and no. This is what is called the 'Eastern Mu'.

The above is an interpretation of Mu arrived at by means of rational inference. It is probably what Master Mumon Yamada calls 'understanding with the head'. It is armchair theory, not what in Zen is known as 'living wisdom'. Just because something has been apprehended with the intellect, it does not necessarily mean that the body and heart go along with that understanding. That is why in most cases, even though we know a thing through intellection, we are

unable to put it into actual practice. Besides, the intellect is
unable to go on grasping this absolute Mu continually, for in
daily life it has to turn its attention to other matters. Therefore we are apt to completely forget about the absolute Mu.
As a result, our understanding of it does not come alive in our
daily life and we end up top-heavy with useless knowledge.

When something is understood with the *hara*, though, it
ought to come alive in one's life, because to apprehend with
the *hara* means to realize with both head and heart, in other
words, with the whole person. In my terminology, it is to
know with the whole 'body'. Mu is to become one with the
other and be concentrated in *samādhi* so that no matter what
you do in daily life, you throw yourself into it body and
soul. This is what is meant by understanding Mu with the
hara and bringing it to life in everyday experience.

Now, in order to truly grasp Mu with the *hara*, you have to
sit up properly, regulate your breath, compose your mind
and become absorbed in one-pointed *samādhi*. But to clear
the mind of all ideas and enter *samādhi*, ordinary effort is not
enough. That is why it is said that you must die the Great
Death with your whole body and soul. Anyone who ever
passed the first barrier had to exhaust every ounce of his
energy in getting through the barrier of the Great Death.

There are also two ways to 'understand' the childlikeness
mentioned by Christ. First, let us listen to what he says
about the mind and heart of a child:

> At that time the disciples came to Jesus saying, 'Who is the greatest
> in the kingdom of heaven?' And calling to him a child, he put him in
> the midst of them, and said, 'Truly, I say to you' unless you turn
> and become like children, you will never enter the kingdom of
> heaven. Whoever humbles himself like this child, he is the greatest
> in the kingdom of heaven' (Matthew 18:1-4).

To 'understand with the head' what it is to have the mind
of a child, is to comprehend this passage by using the knowledge we have gained from Scripture studies. The following
interpretation is an example of this. When the disciples
asked Jesus who was greatest in the kingdom of heaven, in
their hearts was the ambition to become great and surpass
everyone else. In response, Jesus taught them the necessity

of becoming like children. Therefore to have the mind of a child means to be modest and to humble oneself. Without this humility, a person cannot enter heaven, and the one who is most humble will be greatest in heaven. Since this is the case, we must learn to be humble. This is an example of understanding the mind of a child 'with the head'. Yet even though one understands this way 'with the head', if the heart itself continues to be as lax as ever, nothing will come of it. Even though a well-intentioned person, taking this intellectual understanding as a basis, does his utmost to become humble, his heart will not promptly and meekly listen to what his head is telling him. It requires long practice to become humble of heart as well.

Now, what does it mean to understand the mind and heart of a child 'with the *hara*'? It is to realize it with both head and heart, that is, with the whole person. It is to hear the good news of the 'kingdom of heaven' with humility, accept it docilely, and enter into that kingdom with your whole 'body'. When you do that, it will come alive in your daily life. Since to enter the kingdom of heaven is to become a child of the Heavenly Father, not only will your whole 'body' become humble, but you will become simple and unsophisticated, able to open your heart to accept everything. It goes without saying that just as the No-mind of Zen does not mean being apathetic and inert, so having the heart of a child does not mean to be passive and childish. And just as it is necessary to die the Great Death in order to realize the Mu of Zen, so you must throw away everything to become childlike, as I will relate below.

In his commentary on 'Jōshū's dog', Mumon clearly describes the spiritual process of coming to understand Mu with the *hara*. It can be summed up as follows.

The spiritual process of attaining enlightenment

1 'To attain to marvellous enlightenment, you must rid yourself completely of your discriminating mind.' To become enlightened, you must abandon all cognitive and reasoning processes.

2   The concrete way to 'rid yourself completely of your discriminating mind' is to regulate your posture and breathing and to concentrate your attention on 'Mu' as you recite it in your heart.

3   As you do this, questions and doubts will arise. Your whole being must be filled with the question 'What is Mu?' 'Is this "I" Mu?' Mumon describes it thus: 'Then concentrate yourself, with your 360 bones and 84,000 pores, into Mu, making your whole body into one great ball of doubt.'

4   Mu must be present in your mind day and night. Continue to recite it constantly, whether you are doing zazen, eating or resting. Let your whole self be absorbed and concentrated in it. While you are doing this, do not think about whether Mu is nothing or non-being as opposed to being, or an absolute Mu that transcends being and non-being. 'Keep digging into it, day and night, without ceasing. But do not try to take it as nothingness or interpret it dualistically.'

5   If you practise intently like this, after some days it will be 'as though you have gulped down a red-hot iron ball, which you try to vomit up but cannot'. In this complete absorption, self is forgotten and there is no longer any room for ordinary cognitive processes. As you continue in this state, you 'cast away all the delusive thoughts and feelings you have cherished up to now', and your mind becomes increasingly pure and ripe.

6   Then finally, 'Inside and outside will become one naturally.' The distinction between subject and object will disappear, and you will become one with Mu. 'You will be like a dumb person who has had a dream and only knows it for himself.' Just as a dumb person cannot communicate his dream to another, so the only way that you can know it is to have the experience of it yourself.

The real nature of the Mu that is the subject of *satori* (enlightenment) cannot be communicated verbally, no matter how hard one tries. But those who have gone before us on the Way have left many words that may serve as guideposts. I have chosen just two from among them that I would like to use to give some sort of rough sketch of the state called Mu or No-mind in Zen. Master Takuan, in his teachings to Yagyū Tajima no Kami Munenore, says:

The mind of No-mind . . . is by nature never fixed on anything. It is the mind when it has no distinctions, or thoughts, or anything in it. The mind that spreads throughout the body and permeates the whole is called No-mind. It is the mind that has no abode. We call that which, unlike a stone or tree, has no place to stay, No-mind. If it stops somewhere, there is something in the mind, but if it has no stopping place, there is nothing in the mind. We call having nothing in the mind, the mind of No-mind, or No-mind, No-thought . . . .

If one thinks about something in his mind, he does not hear what another is saying even though he listens to him, because his mind is fixed on the thing he is thinking about . . . . This is because there is something in the mind. What is there, is the thought. When you drive the thing that is there away, you turn the mind into No-mind that works only when it has some business to attend to, dealing with the task at hand. The mind that thinks it does not want something to leave it, once again has something in it. But if the mind does not think about it, it leaves of its own accord and the state of No-mind is produced naturally (*Fudōchi Shinmyō-roku* [Admirable Records of Unmoving Wisdom]).

Most people, when they hear 'No-mind', think it means to become unfeeling, like a rock or a tree. But, as Master Takuan teaches us, that is not the case at all. No-mind means not to fix the mind anywhere. For example, when you are facing an opponent in a fight with real swords, No-mind is not to confine your mind anywhere, but to let your energy fill your whole body. If everything in all quarters is uniformly filled with significance and you do not fix your mind on anything, then no matter from which direction your opponent attacks, you will be able to check him with the speed of lightning, and when he has an unguarded moment, you will instantly strike a blow. If, on the contrary, the mind settles in one spot, it will stagnate there and not be watchful in other directions. Then you will present an opening to your opponent and be defeated. If you put your mind on the enemy's sword, it will be held by the sword, and if you place it on the movements of your opponent's body, the mind will be captured by them. Takuan says that you must not think about whether your opponent is strong or you are weak. No-mind is not a vapid state of mind, void of all ideas and thoughts, but rather one in which energy flows through the entire body.

In order to attain this state of mind, it is not enough to

just do zazen vacuously. First, you must sit in dead earnest, exhausting the total energy of your body and soul. Second, you must maintain this same level of energy in your everyday life, throwing your whole self into whatever you do. Not until you devote yourself to this kind of whole-hearted practice, will you be able to say as Master Takuan does:

> When you do not put your mind anywhere it pervades your entire self. And if it has spread through the whole body, when it enters the hand, it does the work of the hand; when it enters the foot, it does the work of the foot; and when it enters the eye, it does the work of the eye. To the extent that it permeates the parts it enters, their functions are fulfilled (*Ibid.*).

Centrifugal and centripetal forces balance out to zero

When I read Master Takuan's explanation of No-mind, I picture to myself the masters of old devoting themselves to strenuous practice and developing the idea of Mu which they passed on to their disciples. What primitive Buddhism grasped as relativity (Sanskrit *śūñyatā*) was transmitted to China where it was apprehended more practically as Mu. Then crossing over to Japan, it developed into the No-mind that came to pervade every nook and cranny of Japanese life. And in modern times, this No-mind has been converted into a more concrete form as the 'state of weightlessness' or zero gravity. My teacher, Master Sōgen Ōmori, has related the following experience to me about No-mind in Japanese fencing:

> I learned the *kata* [form] called *jikishinkageryū no hōjō* from Master Jirokichi Yamada. This *hōjō* is 'to remove all bad habits and addictions acquired since birth and to restore the original pure and bright permanent body.' We might think of the original pure and bright permanent body as what we call one's Primal Face or Mu in Zen. What I am going to relate happened after I had practised this technique for many years and was finally able to perform it freely. One day, as I was practicing this form, my body was filled with energy. All muscular tension left my arms and legs and I became conscious of the fact that the centrifugal and centripetal forces in me had

balanced each other out to zero. It was just as if I were in a state of
weightlessness. Ever since becoming aware of this, I've been able to
achieve this state easily.

Later, when I did zazen and entered *samādhi*, I noticed that just
as when I did this fencing form, the muscular tension left my limbs
and the centrifugal and centripetal forces balanced out to zero. But
it wasn't just a physical balance. I noticed that I had achieved a
balance of the mind, that my spiritual centrifugal and centripetal
forces had likewise balanced each other out. This was a kind of
realization. Afterwards it was very easy for me to reach this state
and I was able to sit very well.

When I heard these recollections from my master, I felt as
though I had been illumined by a great light. He had lucidly
and accurately put into words what I myself had experienced
when doing zazen. I immediately asked him, 'What are these
things you call the centrifugal and centripetal forces of the
mind?' The master pondered this for a while. I impatiently
continued, 'Aren't they the various aspects of our lives that
are in dualistic opposition, such as being and non-being,
subject and object, subjectivity and objectivity, I and you,
enlightenment and delusion, good and evil, beauty and
ugliness, sacred and profane, heaven and earth, activity and
quiescence, one and many, part and whole, joy and sorrow,
sickness and health, poverty and wealth, short life and long,
and so on? Aren't they all the opposites that constitute man
and the world?' The master agreed with me at once.

In Zen, the practitioner is strictly admonished to transcend
all dualistic relativism. And the more he advances, the more
he is ordered thoroughly to break down the dualistic point of
view that remains hidden somewhere in his mind. All of the
koans, but especially the *nantō*, *kōjō* and 'final word' koans
can be said to have this goal. The student must keep pushing
on through with the thought that 'Even Shakyamuni Buddha
and Bodhidharma are still practising. I'm only half way, only
half-way there.'

But in aiming at the transcendence of dualism in the mind,
Zen has had the tendency to be somewhat conceptual and
thus not likely to come alive in everyday life. Occasionally
you hear of cases where even though the person has passed
many koans, Zen is not really alive in his daily life. In order

to make up for this lack, Master Ōmori has introduced
calligraphy and fencing into Zen practice so that Zen will
start to work in the 'body' as well and thus act as an invigor-
ating agent in all the actions of life. I believe that this way of
unified mind-body practice, which has been introduced into
Zen history for the first time by Master Ōmori, can be called
an epoch-making innovation. Through the way of calligraphy,
brush, paper and self become one; free of all restraints, your
whole body is filled with energy and you are able to write
with No-mind. When this is carried over into everyday life,
not only when you take up a pen to write, but also when you
hold a sewing needle or the steering wheel of a car, or do any
other similar kind of work, the creative activity of No-mind
learned through Zen calligraphy comes alive and begins to
function in you.

Like a mirror

I would like to treat briefly one more aspect of No-mind
based on a sermon of Zen Master Bankei, a great and
renowned priest who promoted Unborn Zen. He preached
that each and every one of us has received and possesses an
Unborn Mind:

> The Unborn is like a bright mirror. Even though a mirror doesn't
> try to reflect anything, no matter what comes in front of it, it is
> reflected, isn't it? And even though the mirror doesn't think about
> not reflecting, when the thing in front of it is taken away, it is not
> reflected. What we call the Unborn Mind is just like this. When you
> try to see or hear something, you naturally see and hear it. But even
> when you do not try to see or hear, you do so by virtue of your
> Buddha-nature. This is the Unborn Mind .... If, in listening to
> what I am saying, you understand anything at all, that, in itself, is
> the Buddha-nature (*Bankei Zenji Zen-shu* [Collected Works of
> Bankei] , ed. Kyuji Akao, Daizoshuppan, Tokyo, 1976, p.44).

From ancient times in both East and West, man's mind has
been likened to a mirror. When something comes in front of
it, it is reflected, but when the thing goes away, its image
disappears without leaving a trace. Even though the mirror
may reflect something dirty, it is not soiled. The mind is the

same. If it is not enslaved to anything, it will reflect a thing exactly, but when that thing leaves, its form will not remain. The self is restored to a clean slate and returns to an absolutely new beginning, prepared to reflect accurately all things at any time.

Chapter 10

No-mind and the mind of a child (2)

The teaching of Jesus on childlikeness

Ignatian indifference

The indignation of Jesus

In the previous chapter the Mu of Zen was explained in some detail so the reader should have at least an intellectual grasp of what it is. Now I would like to consider what it means to have the childlike spirit that Christ preached and which is said to resemble this Mu.

Jesus spoke about being childlike on the following occasion:

> And they were bringing children to him, that he might touch them; and the disciples rebuked them. But when Jesus saw it he was indignant, and said to them, 'Let the children come to me, do not hinder them; for to such belongs the kingdom of heaven. Truly, I say to you, whoever does not receive the kingdom of God like a child shall not enter it.' And he took them in his arms and blessed them, laying his hands on them (Mark 10:13-16).

This episode shows clearly the kind of personality that Jesus had. We see that far from being stiff and formal, he was a person whom anyone could approach. The Gospel tells us that before this incident the Pharisees had confronted him with the difficult problem of divorce. Jesus made a clear-cut response in regard to the issue. Then, a number of parents pushed their way through the crowd with their children, hoping to have the famous preacher Jesus lay his hands on them. When the disciples saw this, they probably thought that the people were being a nuisance, for they scolded them sharply. They had not yet acquired the spirit of Jesus. Seeing this, Jesus became very angry with the disciples; the Gospel tells us that he was 'indignant'. In the Greek manuscript for 'indignant' the indefinite form of the verb *aganakteō* is used, which means to be angry, indignant, to take offence at. The disciples must have been very surprised to see Jesus's indignation. The last thing they expected was for him to get angry; they thought that they had done him a service for which he would surely praise them. But instead, Jesus became indignant and said, 'Let the children come to me, do not hinder them.'

The anger of a religious person

We like to think that a great religious person never takes offence or becomes angry. Aren't there many Christians who feel that Jesus, who they believe to be the God-man, would never become indignant? Even though it is plainly recorded in the Gospel that Jesus became angry, they ignore this fact or tend deliberately to avoid talking about it. But the indignation of Jesus has great significance. If we miss its meaning, I doubt whether we can fully grasp his real intention. Well then, why did Jesus become indignant? It wasn't that he gave in to personal feeling and took out his anger on the disciples. Wasn't he indignant, rather, because the disciples had acted contrary to his real spirit and thought that they were doing the right thing? They had gone completely against what Jesus considered was a very important teaching. If he had let it go, the disciples would have completely misinterpreted the good news that he had proclaimed and, from the standpoint of man's salvation, would have handed down a source of woe to posterity. I think Jesus wanted to instil this point into the disciples. For that reason, we can say that his indignation was a manifestation of his ardent desire for the salvation of mankind.

I was given a living instruction on this point by the master from whom I am receiving guidance in Zen. It was when I had first started going to the Tesshū Group Zen *dōjō* (practice hall) every morning, hoping to become a disciple of the master. At that time I had not yet obtained permission to go

to him for private direction. One morning, having finished
our usual zazen, morning sutras and calligraphy, we started to
have ceremonial tea. That day an unusually large number of
disciples were present. Several officers of the Tesshū Group,
including Professor T, Mr O and Mr G, were also in attendance. The master started to speak quietly to a Mr K, saying
that he had heard that someone had asked K to teach him
the *kendo* (swordsmanship) form called *jikishinkageryū* and
that K had gone to that person's home to teach him. Was
that true? the master wanted to know. And had going to this
person's home been K's idea or the other person's? He asked
several such questions, but K was equivocal and avoided
giving him a clear answer.

Then like a thunderbolt, the master castigated K with a
fierce tongue-lashing. Afterwards he said with painstaking
care and patience, 'In the martial arts we do not go to a
student's home to teach. The proper course is for a person
who wants to learn to come to the *dōjō* to study. You're a
practitioner of the martial arts, aren't you? If so, you should
act like one and observe the way strictly.' The master's clear
voice had filled the *dōjō*, piercing the hearts of everyone
present. I started with surprise when I heard it. It was the
most severe reprimand I had ever heard in my life. Never
before or since have I felt so strongly the importance of
observing the way. Reflecting on it now, I realize that the
master's methods of training his disciple by freely 'holding
and releasing' was of no common order. Furthermore, I am
conscious of how much this reprimand was filled with the
master's fervent desire for the salvation of all. Directly
after this incident, I left my place among the others and
went up to the master to ask him to make an inscription on
a box for a piece of calligraphy I had received from him. He
was once again wearing the mild expression he ordinarily did.
I was wide-eyed with astonishment at the sight of his freedom from any attachment to his feelings of a few seconds
before. I doubt whether I shall forget it for as long as I live.
This experience is so deeply rooted in my mind that I can
understand the indignation of Jesus and the disciples' surprise
painfully well. It should be noted that in terms of their
content the words that Jesus spoke following his indignation

had a serene ring to them. We can surmise from this that the tone of Jesus's voice must have been one that quietly penetrated the heart.

The 'wise and understanding' and little children

Let us return to the starting point of this topic. I think it is clear from the above why Jesus was so indignant at the disciples' action; it was because they were deviating from the way that he was trying to teach them. Now, what was this way which he valued so much? He indicates it by his ensuing words, 'Truly, I say to you, whoever does not receive the kingdom of God like a child shall not enter it' (Mark 10:15).

The way to the kingdom of God that Jesus teaches is the way of a child. In the quotation above the word 'receive' is the most important one for an understanding of what that way is. In the Greek manuscript it is the indefinite form of the verb *dexomai*, which means to take something which has been held out, to accept, to receive warmly, to welcome cordially. Thus this sentence is telling us how important it is to welcome from our hearts and docilely accept the 'kingdom of God' that has been offered to us by God the Father. 'Like a child' means to accept someone's kindness docilely, impartially and promptly, without the least bit of doubt or suspicion. If, in addition, we consider the meaning of childlikeness against the background of the good news which Jesus proclaimed, it seems to have an even deeper meaning. As the Scripture scholar J. Jeremias says, it is only a child who, knowing he is safe in God's protection and conscious of his boundless love, can call God *Abba* (dear Father) with childlike confidence.

In connection with this one is reminded of Jesus's prayer on a certain occasion:

> I thank thee, *Abba*, Lord of heaven and earth, that thou hast hidden these things from the wise and understanding and revealed them to babes; yea, *Abba*, for such was thy gracious will (Matthew 11: 25-26).

This prayer shows that Jesus addressed God as dear Father (*Abba*) and that God wills that the 'kingdom of God' proclaimed by Jesus be revealed to 'babes' and hidden from the 'wise and understanding'. 'Babes' and the 'wise and understanding' are set in contraposition, so that if we understand what kind of persons are indicated by the latter term, we will also know what is meant by being a little child. In the time of Christ, 'the wise and understanding' designated teachers or specialists in the law were the Pharisees. Among them were persons who challenged Jesus with malicious questions and tried to trap him because of their zeal for scrupulous observance of the law. They sat in judgment on others, despised sinners and tax collectors, and were only externally devout, forgetting the real spirit of the law. Priding themselves greatly on their knowledge of the law, they looked down on those who were illiterate or of the lower classes. They were scholars: intelligent, clever, and 'questioning in their hearts' (Mark 2:6-8), but they could not meekly accept the 'kingdom of God' that Jesus revealed. The 'babes' placed in contraposition to them, therefore, were ignorant people who knew nothing of the law and were held in contempt by the lawyers, who called them *am ha'aretz* (the poor of the earth).

Throwing away everything

Here one is reminded of the fact that in Zen, also, knowledge is one of the greatest obstacles to practice. Zen stresses that in order to attain enlightenment a person must abandon all concepts and thoughts. It is very interesting that here, too, 'babes' are contrasted with 'the wise and understanding' and indicates a similarity between Zen and Christianity on this point. They can be said to resemble each other in their docile acceptance of things, in reflecting everything as it is like a mirror, without injecting one's personal feelings, in being unhindered by one's knowledge and preconceptions, and in entering into things directly, without chopping logic or quibbling in one's heart.

In addition, Christianity and Zen are similar in one more

important respect. Accepting the kingdom of God docilely, like a child, does not mean to have a wait-and-see attitude of passive acceptance. Rather, it is a positive re-orientation of the whole personality. The following words of Jesus express this very well:

> And calling to him a child, he put him in the midst of them, and said, 'Truly, I say to you, unless you turn and become like children, you will never enter the kingdom of heaven. Whoever humbles himself like this child, he is the greatest in the kingdom of heaven' (Matthew 18:2-4).

We should pay attention to the words 'turn and become like children' in this passage. In the original, 'turn' is *strephō*, which means to change, turn, to turn one's head, to convert. The indefinite passive form means to turn one's self, alter one's direction, have a change of heart, turn over a new leaf, and so on. With these words Jesus wants to stress that we must make a radical turnabout in our manner of living and 'become like children'. When we think about it, we realize that we have completely lost the heart of a little child that we were born with. Driven by our likes and dislikes, we can no longer docilely accept things as they are. It is clear that we will never become like little children in our present condition; no one will deny that a conversion of one's whole self is necessary before this is possible.

Again, Jesus teaches this with an especially skilful parable:

> The kingdom of heaven is like treasure hidden in a field, which a man found and covered up; then in his joy he goes and sells all that he has and buys that field (Matthew 13:44).

Here the kingdom of God is called the kingdom of heaven but it means the same thing. In order to receive the kingdom of God, one must go home in joy and sell all he has; what is demanded here is complete abandonment. One must return to his own self and then abandon that self with all the strength of his mind and body. To accept the kingdom of God means to hurl your entire energy into giving up your ego. Perhaps that is why Jesus said, 'From the days of John the Baptist until now the kingdom of heaven has suffered violence, and men of violence take it by force' (Matthew

11:12). This resembles the Zen teaching that in order to realize Mu one must exhaust the entire energy of mind and body in throwing away everything and dying the Great Death. As I mentioned before, zazen is not passive meditation, but an extremely positive self-abandonment of body and mind. The Deva King Zen advocated by Master Shōsan Suzuki shows this so directly. Deva King Zen teaches that aimless and carefree sitting is not enough to enable us to rise above the world. We must root out our passions and sit with an intrepid spirit and the vigour of the fierce Deva Kings who stand as guardians at temple gates.

Men of later generations who inherited Jesus's teaching about the heart of a child expanded it in various concrete ways. Francis of Assisi developed it in the direction of simple holy poverty; Teresa of Avila and John of the Cross in the way 'all or nothing' of perfect renunciation; Thérèse, the Little Flower, in the way of the little one, and Ignatius of Loyola in the way of indifference. Here, I would like to comment on just one of them, the spirit of Ignatian indifference. In some respects it resembles the No-mind of Zen.

Ignatian spirituality

Among the writings of Ignatius Loyola there is a book called *The Spiritual Exercises*. In the third part of the present work, I will be discussing the similarities between the *Spiritual Exercises* and a Zen *sesshin* and will go into the background of Ignatius's book there. In the beginning of the book the 'principle and foundation' of the Christian life is explained. According to this explanation, 'Man is created to praise, reverence, and serve God our Lord, and by this means to save his soul. All other things on the face of the earth are created for man to help him fulfill the end for which he is created.' These words express the Christian view of life and the world. It hardly need be mentioned that it is entirely different from the outlook on life and the world found in Mahayana Buddhism, which constitutes the background of Zen. This is an ideological difference, but what if we were to compare them in terms of religious practice? How do they actually differ when it comes to the case of someone who is practising intently and has abandoned all intellection? How do they differ in their existential orientation? And if we say there are similarities between them, in just what points do they resemble each other?

In both Zen and Christianity, when a person has to make an important leap during the course of practice, he must separate himself from all conscious ideas. As we saw above in Mumon's description of the koan 'Jōshū's Dog', in order to achieve a Zen enlightenment 'You must rid yourself completely of your discriminating mind'. The same thing can be said in the case of Christian contemplation. John of the Cross speaks of the 'night of the senses' and the 'night of the soul' and says that in order to attain to a deep mystical experience, you must quiet all movements of the senses and of the soul and treat the 'light of natural reason' as if it did not exist.

> And thus a soul is greatly impeded from reaching this high state of union with God when it clings to any understanding or feeling or imagination or appearance or will or manner of its own, and cannot detach and strip itself of all these . . . and thus a soul must pass beyond everything to unknowing (*Ascent of Mount Carmel*).

Now then, what if we compare the existential orientations that remain in Christianity and Zen after the practitioner has dispelled all concepts? Speaking from my own meagre experience, I would say the two differ in a fine point regarding their ultimate aims, but that in regard to their overall framework and structure they are very similar. I would like to leave an examination of these points of difference and similarity to an investigation into practice that I will be making in the future. Here, I would just like to add that the Christian 'Lord God', as I will mention in the third part of this book, is not something that can become the object of man's consciousness. Consequently, God cannot, as most people including Christians think, be the object of human rational understanding nor be apprehended by it. If we have the premise in our heads 'God is — (infinite and all good, for example)' that is already a designation of something that is not God. For instance, if we say, 'God is omnipotent and omniscient', we must immediately add that God cannot be completely apprehended by such a notion. As a number of my Christian friends have put it, when we pray, God is not an object opposite us but a person who prays with us. In other words, we are enveloped in that person and pray by his direct action. To put it in Zen terms, we pray becoming one with God. This is the ideal of Christian prayer. A god that has descended to the level of something relative to us is not the real God. God absolutely transcends all relativity to creatures. He is beyond the imagination of the human intellect. He envelops us and is immanent in us.

Transcending dualistic relativism

Returning to our original topic, Ignatius, after explaining man's goal in 'Principle and Foundation', writes the following. There is something in it that is very similar to the No-mind of Zen:

> From this it follows that man is to use these things to the extent that they will help him to attain his end. Likewise, he must rid himself of them in so far as they prevent him from attaining it. Therefore we must make ourselves indifferent to all created things, in so far as it is left to the choice of our free will and is not forbidden. Acting accordingly, for our part, we should not prefer health to sickness, riches to poverty, honour to dishonour, a long life to a short one, and so in all things we should desire and choose only those things which will best help us attain the end for which we are created (Exercise 23).

Ignatian indifference has both negative and positive aspects. It is negative in respect to not being inclined toward either alternative, i.e., sickness or health, poverty or riches, a short life or a long one. This is the aspect referred to by Master Takuan as 'not fixing the mind anywhere'. Indifference here does not mean 'to have the attitude of a passive observer'. The essential element of Ignatian indifference is to always have the attitude of desiring only those things which will lead us closer to our ultimate goal. The words that deserve special attention here are 'We should desire and choose *only* (*solamente*) those things which will *best* (*mas*) help us attain the end for which we are created.' They clearly reveal the positiveness and devotedness of Ignatian spirituality. In this connection, it is worth mentioning that Ignatian spirituality attaches special importance to the concrete acts of daily life and that it tries to transform them into acts of religious practice. On this point it greatly resembles Zen, and it is very close to Rinzai Zen in its positiveness and practicality.

Now, I believe that this Ignatian indifference is similar to the transcendence of dualistic relativism in Zen that I spoke of above. As was mentioned, it is to transcend the centrifugal and centripetal forces of the soul, that is, all things that are dualistically relative, such as being and nothingness, good and evil, sickness and health, poverty and wealth, and so on, so that 'though remaining in the world, the world of discrimination, one is always living in the absolute world' (conversation with Master Sōgen). In Ignatian terms, it is to transcend the dualistic opposition of sickness and health, poverty and wealth, contempt and honour, short life and long, always maintaining a spirit of indifference. Then, though remaining in the world of discrimination in all things, one rises above it and lives (in the absolute world of) praising and serving God, who is the Goal of all creation. I believe it can be said with certainty that these definite points of similarity exist between the two.

Points of difference

In the two preceding chapters, we have considered the No-mind of Zen and the childlikeness preached by Jesus, pointing out the similarities between them. As should be clear from the above description, they greatly resemble each other in terms of their basic attitudes. In two or three important respects, however, they are dissimilar.

In the first place, let me point out a superior point of the Zen No-mind that has thus far been lacking in Christianity. This is the concrete method of practising to achieve No-mind. The training of the whole person by means of zazen and working on koans had its source in the Yoga of ancient India.

It was further developed through the devoted practice of Eastern peoples over a period of five or six thousand years. Thus it stands to reason that it is an outstanding way of religious practice. I firmly believe that henceforth Christianity must learn much from Zen on this point. We would do well to pay attention to the fact that in Japan practising with the whole body and soul has been embodied in everyday life and has even developed into the swordsmanship and calligraphy of Masters Takuan and Ōmori. Accordingly, the spirit of Mu that developed in Chinese Zen has been given new life and realized in more concrete form. In this respect we Christians have much to learn from Zen.

Another difference is that there is something in the Christian childlikeness that is not found in the No-mind of Zen. What Jesus called becoming like a child is, first of all, to have the heart of a little child in respect to God the Father. God invites all men to his own 'kingdom of God' with the spirit of a Father. A person who accepts this invitation docilely has the heart of a little child. Only a child can be sensitive to God's infinite love and call God 'Father' with the utmost confidence. This is the spirit of love of father and child.

Jesus himself was a child in respect to God. It is written in the Bible that he burned with zeal for his Father's house, but as the only Son of God the Father, he had the heart of a child towards God. It was in conformity with this spirit that he told us to 'become like children'. Childlikeness was an essential quality of Jesus from the outset and reveals his basic attitude towards God the Father. His teaching about little children is the overflowing of this intrinsic quality. The 'rivers of living water' (John 7:38) which flowed from Jesus will flow out of our hearts (*Ibid.*) and impel us to become little children in respect to God the Father.

Mark's Gospel says that after Jesus preached about becoming childlike, he embraced the little children. This drawing the little children to his breast is not just an expression of his love for them, but it also symbolizes forcefully his deep connection to, or rather, his spiritual identity with them.

Chapter 11

The mystery of words

'Unmon's dried shit stick' (*Mumonkan*, Case 21)

Blessed are the poor (Luke 6:20)

'Unmon's dried shit stick'

Zen koans are generally so paradoxical that they are beyond the comprehension of the ordinary person. The Zen master may use them to go directly contrary to the hearer's expectations, and they often come out in unexpected words and actions which may even trap the hearer in an enigma. A typical example is the koan called 'Unmon's dried shit stick'.

> A monk inquired earnestly of Unmon, 'What is Buddha?' Unmon said, 'A dried shit stick' (*Mumonkan*, Case 21).

A shit stick was used in ancient China for scraping up dung. Most people think of the Buddha as something pure, and the monk who asked this question most probably did too. But Unmon went directly against this idea and replied, 'A dried shit stick.' When he heard this the monk was struck dumb with surprise. Now, why did Unmon make such an answer?

Traditionally it has been said that each of Unmon's replies contains three functions; they are known as: (1) 'the box and lid, heaven and earth'; (2) 'cutting off the flow of delusions'; (3) 'waves following waves'. The first of these means that when the questioner makes his inquiry with heaven, Unmon responds with earth, and when he asks with a box,

93

the reply is made with the lid. Unmon's reply, 'A dried shit stick', is a good example of this. To the monk who thinks Buddha is something pure, he replies with a filthy shit stick. But why did Unmon make such an eccentric response? The reason is indicated by the phrase 'cutting off the flow of delusions'. With his curious reply, Unmon instantly cut off the flow of delusion in the monk and tried to effect a conversion of his complete existence. Yet what is so surprising is that this reply by Unmon, which at first seems so bizarre, is none the less a proper answer to the monk's question. This is what is meant by the phrase 'waves following waves': just as one wave follows on another, the proper answer follows upon the question.

Putting an end to life

Zen koans press the practitioner to make a great conversion so that he will die to his habitual way of thinking and living and be reborn on a new plane. For that reason, a koan is both a killing and a life-giving sword. This is true also of 'Unmon's dried shit stick'. Thinking about the meaning of a dried shit stick or trying to discover a significant relationship between it and the Buddha-nature will not solve the koan. Nor is there any use in looking for some hidden or figurative meaning in the koan. Completely unrelated as it is to anything a person normally expects, a koan confronts the practitioner like an insurmountable wall. Through it, the life breath of the practitioner's delusive self is cut off and he is made to change his previous way of life.

This is accompanied, furthermore, by the activity of the killing sword brandished by the master. A koan is not something that you are at liberty to read and respond to by yourself. You receive a koan from the master and the next time you come before him for *dokusan*, you must present your grasp of its essential points to him. A good master will make an accurate judgment of this presentation and reject anything that is not right. If your understanding is an answer that you have come to intellectually, you can be sure that it will be flatly refused. In some cases, every time a student presents an answer in *dokusan* it is rejected by the master. Finally he is stripped of everything and driven into a corner. All avenues of escape are cut off and his situation is desperate. There is no other way to extricate himself from this situation than to go beyond himself. He must overthrow his former way of thinking and living and, transcending the state of his narrow self, leap onto a higher plane.

When viewed superficially, the asking and answering of koans seems to be related only to the objective world, and a person may think that talking about Buddha or a dried shit stick has no connection to him personally. But actually these are the practitioner's own problems. Am I really Buddha? Is this self of mine, which is as filthy as a shit stick, really Buddha? This is what the koan is aiming at. As long as the koan does not become your own problem, you will never be able to solve it. In Zen, it is often said that the answer is in the question. When the inquirer becomes the question itself, the question disappears. What Zen calls one's Primal Face or Buddha-nature is infinite and inexplicable; in other words, it is the question itself. Thus when the inquirer completely becomes the question, the Buddha-nature is manifested and the question is resolved of its own accord. The same situation can be described from another point of view as follows: the Buddha-nature is asleep in the depths of your unconscious, but when you become the question itself, the Buddha-nature awakens in the innermost recesses of your mind and manifests itself in its entirety. When that happens you realize clearly that your self, which seems to you to be a shit stick, just as it is is living the life of Buddha. You will become aware that you are standing right in the middle of the reality that all creation lives by the life of Buddha.

Approaching the inexplicable

This kind of reflection shows us that Unmon's response, which seemed to be a contradiction at first, is an exceedingly appropriate answer. Thrusting a dirty-looking shit stick before the eyes of his inquirer, Unmon presses him again and again, 'Look, look! The Buddha-life is alive right here! That bag of manure you call a body lives by the life of Buddha! Well? Do you understand?' If, instead of replying directly, Unmon had explained, 'All being is kept in existence by the life of Buddha; therefore, a dried shit stick is endowed with the Buddha-nature and it goes without saying that your body is, too', the questioner may have apprehended it intellectually and felt he understood, but it would never have become a wisdom that he could vigorously put to practical use in everyday life. When we see something filthy or come in contact with a person who has faults or sins, we may be repelled or seized by feelings of disgust which we cannot shake off. No matter how much we think, 'That thing, too, is endowed with the Buddha-nature', or 'All sentient beings are intrinsically Buddha', we are unable to detach ourselves from our feelings of dislike.

What must be realized is that this unclean self of mine, as well as everything that is, no matter how filthy it may look, harbours the life of Buddha, and that in this Buddha-life all being is one. But it is not enough to know this conceptually; you must experience it with your 'body'. This kind of realization is called an unthought thought, impossible to express no matter how exhaustively you explain it. Indeed, the more one tries to make a verbal explanation of the unthought thought, the more the listener will try to understand it intellectually and the further he will draw away from it. To lead someone to this unthought thought and bring him to witness the Buddha-nature directly, the more concise you are the better it is. In this sense as well, Unmon's reply can be called very appropriate. We should also note that Unmon replies with a concrete thing like a dried shit stick; the truth to be realized in Zen is not an abstract principle but the concrete fact as it is.

Blessed are the poor

Among the words of Jesus there are some that, like Unmon's shit stick, are paradoxical and extremely difficult to understand. In certain cases they go directly opposite to what we think and take us by surprise. The opening words of the Sermon on the Mount are an example:

Blessed are you poor, for yours is the kingdom of God.
Blessed are you that hunger now, for you shall be satisfied.
Blessed are you that weep now, for you shall laugh.
Blessed are you when men hate you, and when they exclude you and
   revile you, and cast out your name as evil, on account of the Son
   of man!
Rejoice in that day, and leap for joy, for behold, your reward is
   great in heaven; for so their fathers did to the prophets.
But woe to you that are rich, for you have received your consolation.
Woe to you that are full now, for you shall hunger.
Woe to you that laugh now, for you shall mourn and weep.
Woe to you, when all men speak well of you, for so their fathers did
   to the false prophets (Luke 6:20-26).

Our common sense tells us that the rich are fortunate and
the poor unfortunate, that the person who has eaten his fill is
happy and the hungry man is unhappy. Yet Jesus says that
the poor are fortunate and the rich unfortunate, that the
hungry are blessed and those who have eaten their fill unfortunate. When a man of common sense says 'heaven', Jesus
responds with 'earth'. The persons who heard this sermon
must have been stunned. Jesus's words appear to have the
exact same function as the 'box and cover, heaven and earth'
activity of Unmon's speech. But why did Jesus indulge in
such paradoxical language? Wasn't it because he wanted to
change radically the listeners' way of thinking and living? I
wonder if it is reading too much into it to see here also the
activity of Unmon's 'cutting off the flow of delusions'?
   The Gospel quotes twice (Luke 4:18 and Matthew 11:5)
the words of Isaiah (61:1), 'The Lord has anointed me to
bring good things to the afflicted', in telling us that Jesus's
mission was to bring the good news of the kingdom of God
to the needy. In fact the people who gathered around Jesus
were, for the most part, the poor and humble (Matthew
11:25; John 7:48). Jesus himself was one of the poor. Born
in a stable in Bethlehem, he was raised as the son of a car-
penter, and during his missionary life he lived in such poverty
that he could say, 'Foxes have holes, and birds of the air
have nests; but the son of man has nowhere to lay his head'
(Matthew 8:20). This experience must have given him an
appreciation of the blessing of being poor, for it was by this

poverty that he personally embodied the manifestation of the
'kingdom of God'. In fact, his words 'Blessed are you poor,
for yours is the kingdom of God' are a truth that is realized
first of all in Jesus himself. Nothing touches our hearts more
than the words of someone who has actually experienced
what he is talking about. I think that anyone who listens to
these words of Jesus with his whole body and soul will be
greatly shocked, and the words will be so deeply burned into
his mind that he will never be able to forget them.

The word of God is a two-edged sword

No amount of pondering over it will help us to understand
how poverty is related to happiness. In fact, the more we
think about it, the less we may understand it. Even with a
background in theology, trying to reflect on the relation
between poverty and the kingdom of God will not bring one
to true happiness. Unless you actually experience poverty
and put yourself completely in the kingdom of God, Jesus's
words will not come alive for you. How many Christians
there are who advocate holy poverty, meditate on it, and
build up a wonderful theology of the kingdom of God, but
cannot appreciate the true happiness of it because they are
not bodily living a life of poverty.

Like a Zen koan, the words of Jesus impel us towards a
great conversion, so that dying to our present way of thinking and living, we are brought to life in a poor and blessed
state of realization. In that sense, Jesus's words are a killing
and a life-giving sword. They have this kind of living power
intrinsically, but because we try to make meaningful connec-
tions between poverty, the kingdom of God and happiness,
and show how they are consistent, we end up smothering
the killing and life-giving power of Jesus's words. If we were
to listen intently with No-mind to the Sermon on the Mount,
which is so different from anything we might expect to hear,
it will confront us like 'a silver mountain or a wall of iron'.
In other words, if, instead of listening to Christ's words with
our heads, we take them in with the *hara* and leave everything to their intrinsic power to shock, our previous way of

thinking and living will be transformed by them. In the Bible, the word of God is likened to a two-edged sword:

> For the word of God is living and active, sharper than any two-edged sword, piercing to the division of soul and spirit, of joints and marrow, and discerning thoughts and intentions of the heart (Hebrews 4:12).

John, who shared a life of poverty with Jesus, says he saw 'eternal life' manifested in his personality (1 John 1:2), and that Jesus was the Word of God who 'became flesh and dwelt among us' (John 1:14). If this testimony by John is true, then we can say that Jesus's words have a power which is more piercing than any two-edged sword.

Towards true happiness

The words of Jesus are, moreover, 'living and active'; that is, they are a life-giving sword. They have the mysterious power to rouse the hearer to desire poverty and obtain true happiness. This hidden attraction may be the reason the Bible has continued to be a best seller for two thousand years. All people, without exception, want to become happy, but they do not know where real happiness lies, and so they devote themselves to the pursuit of wealth, honour and high social standing. To all of us who have lost our way, Jesus indicates where true happiness can be found. He teaches us that attachment to material wealth leads to unhappiness and that abandoning such wealth is the way to happiness. In that sense, Jesus's words are a response to a desire in our hearts. I think that here we have the working of 'waves following waves', as in the case of Unmon's phrases.

The poverty that is being preached by Christ means being 'poor in spirit', as Matthew says (5:3), and is not the result of idleness or squandering. Nor does it mean a negative poverty that reluctantly endures straitened circumstances. It connotes, rather a positive poverty that the Spirit moves one to accept voluntarily. It is the refreshing state in which rather than being resigned to poverty, one regards it as one's fortune. At the bottom of this conviction there breathes the secret belief that if a person takes this road that Jesus walked, he will never be abandoned by the heavenly Father.

> Therefore do not be anxious, saying, 'What shall we eat?' or 'What shall we drink?' or 'What shall we wear?' For the Gentiles seek all these things; and your heavenly Father knows that you need them all (Matthew 6:31-32).

The advantage of beginning life with nothing

In connection with these words of Jesus, I am reminded of something Master Mumon Yamada said. Though the quotation is rather long, I would like to reprint it in full here because it is a living commentary on Jesus's words. I hope that it will be read while keeping in mind the childlikeness and No-mind of the previous chapter:

> It is said that you must have the No-mind of an infant, but if immediately you wonder how you will be able to live in this hard world with the carefree mind of a baby, things don't go well. And it is said that if you don't think about it, you will come off a loser every day. So what should you do? Actually, I think it is because you think about it that it becomes hard to live, and when you don't think about it, things become much easier. . . .
>
> We were all born stark-naked, not thinking about anything or setting up projects or plans or making a budget. There has never been a new-born babe who came out carrying a suitcase. All of them are stark-naked, without even a supply of diapers. And although they are coming into a world whose assistance they will be receiving for decades, they don't even bring a hand towel as a calling present. They start life with nothing but their own bodies. Yet isn't the fact that we have lived this long due to the help of others? We are not able to survive because of our own thinking about it. It is thanks to other persons, isn't it, that we have been allowed to get along thus far?
>
> When a baby is born, there is milk from its mother's breast all ready for it. The milk comes from the mother, but it is useless for her. It is to be given to the baby. No matter how much you would like to feed an infant beefsteak because it is so nutritious, it won't eat it. As soon as it is born, the baby is provided with that splendid thing called milk, which becomes thicker as the baby grows. When

the child becomes able to eat solids, his teeth come in. From birth he is in a world which is set up for living and so he can live. 'Look at the birds of the air: they neither sow nor reap but God feeds them.' 'O you of little faith, do not be anxious about what you will wear or what you will eat.' A person is made in such a way that once he is born, he can survive (*Mumon Hōwa-shū* [Mumon's Dharma Talks], Shunjūsha, Tokyo, 1972, p.47).

What Christian reverberations there are in this sermon by Master Mumon!

Chapter 12

The way you live is the way you die

Life and death itself is the life of the Buddha
(Dōgen)

Look at the birds of the air (Matthew 6:26)

The Shōbōgenzō *(The Eye and Treasury of the True Law)*
is a koan

Master Sōgen Ōmori once told me, 'Each passage of Dōgen Zenji's *Shōbōgenzō* is a koan. You should put your whole body and soul into seriously studying it.' I have kept this instruction in my heart, and when I read the *Shōbōgenzō*, I try not to read it with my head. Just as when tackling a koan, I unify my mind and body through zazen and, attaining *prajñā* wisdom, endeavour to read the *Shōbōgenzō* with that eye.

Among the chapters I have read in this way, there is one entitled 'Life and Death' that I especially like to read over and over again. It is said that this chapter was originally an instruction to government officials and warriors, which may account for its being written in a way that is easy for the layman to understand. The contents are an expression of Dōgen's religious experience and strike at its core extraordinarily well. In 'Life and Death' we find the following:

> Life and death itself is the life of the Buddha. If you hate and reject it, you lose the life of Buddha. And if you are attached to life and death, you also lose the life of Buddha. You are stopping at mere outer appearances. It is only when you neither hate nor desire it that you will be able to enter the mind of Buddha.

Every time I read these words of Dōgen Zenji they seem to bore into me more deeply. Once when I was reading them, I recalled some other words that had affected me in the same way. It was a remark made by a Christian that I think has something in common with Dōgen's view of life and death.

Man dies in the same way that he lives

There is an Italian Brother named D in our house who for the past forty years has been silently caring for the sick in Jesuit houses. A cheerful person, Brother D has a good sense of humour, and although he can be a bit of a cynic, he is also very considerate. When I talk to him, I always feel light-hearted. Once this man made the following remarks to me:

> I have encountered many Jesuits in the Society over the years. Among them were men who were revered as saints as well as some who were selfish and hard to handle. There were famous preachers such as Peter Lombardi and unknown priests who spent a quiet life within the monastery like Father Vecqueray who died recently in this house. There were world-famous scholars as well as brothers who worked in the kitchen their whole lives. I've been infirmarian in both Italy and Japan and have been able to observe at close hand how people behave when they get sick and how they meet their death. From that experience I've come to the following conclusion: *quale vita, tale morte* (a man dies in the same way that he lives).

Being infirmarian is an inconspicuous job that requires a great deal of patience. These words came from Brother D's forty long, hard years as infirmarian. When I first heard them from his mouth they made a strong impact on me, and although nearly two years have passed since then, they are impressed on my mind as freshly now as the moment I heard them.

Is this world a tunnel to heaven?

There are some Christians who think that this world is a tunnel to heaven. For them, earth is a place of exile and heaven is their true home. They see this world as a temporary abode, full of suffering, and believe that they only have to go to the next world to find true happiness. It is just a matter of being patient for a while; if only they can endure their passage through this dark tunnel, they will soon find themselves in the brightness of heaven.

At first glance, this kind of thinking seems to be Christian. In one of the prayers to the Blessed Mother we have the passage 'to thee do we turn in our sighs, mourning and weeping in this valley of tears'. But if we put too much stress on the fact that this world is a journey and deny its positive meaning, we are in danger of falling into error. Christ's revelation tells us 'the kingdom of God' is already being realized in this world; and it is a reality that 'we should be called children of God; and so we are' (1 John 3:1).

Life in this world, therefore, is not simply a 'temporary abode' that will pass away; it is already 'the kingdom of God', 'the kingdom of heaven' (Matthew 10:7). Without a recognition of this kind of positive value in our worldly existence, the ideas mentioned above cannot be called truly Christian.

Life and death are both the life of God

To put it another way, it is a mistake to think that this world is only a place to pile up merit in order to enter heaven and that it lacks any value in itself. The 'kingdom of God' is already being realized in our present life and the glory of God shines forth in it. Therefore to live in this world has a positive meaning in itself.

I think it was St Ireneaus who said, 'The glory of God is man himself fully alive.' These words are continually being realized in this world and will be fully disclosed in heaven after death (1 John 3:2). God's life has already been bestowed on us and this will be manifested at our death. Consequently life and death are both the life of God.

The words of Brother D, 'Quale vita, tale morte', mean also that a person's death is of the same quality as his life. That, of course, is no coincidence. We have seen above that life after death is a leaping extension (a non-continuous continuation) of life in this world. They are two different manifestations of the same divine life. To borrow Dōgen's idea quoted earlier, this world, life and death are all the life of God. If you hate them and try to reject them, you lose the life of God. Conversely, if you are attached to life in this world, you are caught up with only the appearances of God's life and you lose the life of God.

If we realize this, there is no need to live in fear of death or to be pessimistic about this world. Didn't Christ also say, 'Whoever would save his life will lose it' (Matthew 16:25)?

In this connection, the following sermon of Jesus is also brought to mind. It is so simple that anyone can understand it, but to comprehend its real meaning and to be able to live the life of God is not such an easy matter.

Look at the birds of the air: they neither sow nor reap nor gather into barns, and yet your heavenly Father feeds them. Are you not of more value than they? And which of you by being anxious can add one cubit to his span of life? And why are you anxious about clothing? Consider the lilies of the field, how they grow; they neither toil nor spin; yet I tell you, even Solomon in all his glory was not arrayed like one of these. But if God so clothes the grass of the field, which today is alive and tomorrow is thrown into the oven, will he not much more clothe you, O men of little faith? Therefore do not be anxious, saying, 'What shall we eat?' or 'What shall we drink?' or 'What shall we wear?' For the Gentiles seek all these things; and your heavenly Father knows that you need them all. But seek first his kingdom and his righteousness, and all these things shall be yours as well (Matthew 6:26-33).

The meaning of 'look'

The above passage opens with the words 'Look at the birds of the air'. The 'look' is important. The Greek manuscript has the indefinite imperative of *emblépo* which means to look well, to see into the heart of, to penetrate the real state of affairs. It resembles very much the way Zen masters use the word 'look' in their sermons and *dokusan*. For instance, when giving the student a koan, a master will tell him to look at koan such-and-such. In this case 'look' means to mobilize one's whole body and soul in grappling with the koan and then to look with the eye of wisdom that is born of that practice. When we encounter Jesus's admonition to 'look' in the Bible, we should not think about his words with our heads, but throw our whole selves into listening to them.

Ordinarily we look at things absent-mindedly. It has become difficult recently to find the 'birds of the air' in metropolitan areas, but we can still see some sparrows and crows in downtown Tokyo. Yet even if we catch sight of them, we tend to look at them absent-mindedly and so are incapable of seeing the sacredness of the life there. If we look carefully, however, we notice that in spite of the polluted atmosphere, the sparrows are chirping and the crows cawing as they fly about the busy streets. There is a small garden beside our house. Although it is right in the middle of Tokyo, each morning and evening several kinds of small birds visit it, delighting our ears with their clear songs. Every time I hear the beautiful warbling of these little birds, I marvel at the mystery of life. When I reflect on it deeply, I realize what a surprising thing the life of the 'birds of the air' is. Isn't divine life breathing there? And when I realize that this great divine life that is keeping the little birds alive is also animating me in the same way, I am permeated with a sense of the holiness and wonder of life.

Not long ago, in the Sophia University Lecture Series, Shōichi Yamazaki, honorary professor of Tokyo University, gave a lecture entitled 'About Death'. He said:

> Modern man sees only the phenomena that occur before his eyes. He doesn't try to understand the deeper meaning behind these phenomena. In regard to death, also, modern man pays attention only to the external phenomena. Breathing stops, the body becomes cold, is cremated and becomes ashes. That's all there is. Man doesn't try to see the world behind death, the world of the true meaning of death. We can say the same thing about life.

I think the same thing can be said about the 'birds of the air'. When modern man sees birds flying in the air, he only sees the external phenomena. About as far as he goes is to think that the sparrow chirping from its perch on a telephone pole is a pathetic sight, scrawny and soot-covered as a result of air pollution. He does not see the life force that has managed not to succumb to the pollution, much less feel the breath of the divine life there. And he probably laughs off as childish sentimentalism the thought of seeing God's life in the life of a little bird.

The sages of old, however, who practised 'letting go of mind and body' saw 'great life' in all living things. Looking again at the words of Dōgen Zenji quoted at the beginning of this chapter, we see that he asserts positively, 'Life and death itself is the life of the Buddha.' The life of a sparrow, as well as its death, is the life of the great Enlightened One. How much more is that true of the life of a person?

The birds of the air are the life of God; the lilies of the field are the life of God; our life and death is the life of God. What is there to worry about? To throw off mind and body and fling one's self into the 'kingdom of God', to put all one's might into living in whatever way the life that comes from God impels us — isn't that the very thing that Jesus is teaching us in the sermon above?

We are already the children of God who are waiting for the revelation of that fact. To live a creative life with the freedom of the children of God — that is the Christian reality.

In his second childhood — the charismatic 'figure' of Bishop Ross

There was more to Brother D's story. He went on to talk about Bishop Ross who died in December of 1969. For eleven years Bishop Ross had carried out the responsible duties of head of the Hiroshima Diocese. When the Second World War began, he turned the diocese over to a Japanese bishop and retired. From then on he lived the life of an ordinary member of a Jesuit house.

After the war, Bishop Ross taught Latin to the seminarians for many years, never giving any indication that he was proud of being a bishop. Twice a week he would clean the house toilets, trying not to let this be seen by others, and continued to do so until late in life. Eventually he had a cerebral haemorrhage which paralysed half his body and impaired his speech.

Brother D continued, 'The last few years of his life, Bishop Ross was a patient at Blessed Mother Hospital in Tokyo. Something surprising happened while he was there. This half-paralysed patient who couldn't speak was exerting a great spiritual influence on a large number of persons. His eyes, bright as a child's, his kind smile and good humour completely captured the hearts of the Sisters and nurses and doctors who cared for him. Our Jesuit superior was afraid that the bishop was a bother to the hospital staff and wanted to have him brought back to a Jesuit house. But do you know what happened? The Sisters at the hospital insisted he wasn't a bit of trouble and begged that he be allowed to stay. As a matter of fact, I heard that one of the doctors decided to become a Christian after coming in contact with the bishop's silent example.'

I was one of Bishop Ross's Latin students for a year before I entered the Society of Jesus. He taught our lazy and dull-witted class with great energy and patience. Teaching Latin can hardly be called a job appropriate for a bishop. Bishop Ross not only did it joyfully, but he also seemed to have a strong sense of dedication to his job of teaching candidates for the priesthood.

I was deeply moved when Brother D told me about Bishop Ross last year. He was physically incapacitated and his brain deteriorating, and yet the 'body' of Bishop Ross radiated a lofty spirituality that was capable of touching the hearts of others. No one has demonstrated more admirably how the 'body' speaks with greater eloquence than any words. What the modern Japanese respect most is a high IQ, a good memory, and the ability to act rationally. All of this had been taken away from Bishop Ross, and yet as a human being he was able to teach something extremely valuable to others. Isn't the charismatic 'figure' of the senile Bishop Ross a stringent warning to us modern Japanese?

When I close my eyes, there floats before them the figure of the aged, cheerful Bishop Ross smiling to a nurse in his room at Blessed Mother Hospital. Then the figure of him enthusiastically teaching Latin in a shabby classroom at Sophia University is superimposed on it, forming a double image that continues, even now, to teach me what it means to live.

Chapter 13

Doing religious reading with the 'body'

All is the living body-mind of the Buddha
and Patriarchs (Dōgen)

This is my body (Matthew 26:26)

The living body-mind of the Buddha and Patriarchs

The following is one of my favourite sayings of Dōgen Zenji:
'Each and every line of the sutras is the living body-mind of
the Buddha and Patriarchs.' Dōgen's central thought regarding the Buddhist scriptures is revealed in these words.

Ordinarily in Zen, not much emphasis is put on studying
the sutras and teachings of the Patriarchs because it fills the
head with intellectual knowledge that becomes an obstacle to
achieving a deep religious experience. That was also the
thinking of Dōgen Zenji. Therefore he strictly warns his
disciples not to be caught up by the words of the sutras or to
study them conceptually. Yet, at the same time, he teaches
that the proper reading of the sutras is indispensible to the
practice of Zen:

> When students are first moved to study Buddhism, they should look
> at the sutras and treatises and study them thoroughly, regardless of
> whether they have the mind that seeks the Way or not (*Shōbōgenzō
> Zuimonki*, Ch. 4, No. 8).

> Both the Buddhist sutras and the words of the Patriarchs are genuine
> transmissions from Shakyamuni Buddha.... If, as you say, we
> should throw away the sutras, we must also reject the mind of
> Buddha and the body of Buddha. And if we reject the mind and
> body of Buddha, we must also reject the disciples of Buddha. And if

we reject the disciples of Buddha, it means rejecting the Way of
Buddha. If we reject the Way of Buddha, we are also rejecting the
Way of the Patriarchs (*Shōbōgenzō*, 'Bukkyō' [Buddhist Sutras]).

According to Dōgen Zenji, there is no Buddhist Way, no
Way transmitted from master to disciple, without the
Buddhist sutras. What is most remarkable in this passage is
that it teaches a kind of identity of Buddhism and the body-
mind of Buddha. Ordinary literary works may be products
of the writer's spirit and mind, but the Buddhist scriptures
come not only from the mind of Buddha but also from his
religious practice into which he has put his whole body and
mind. Thus it is only proper that we should see the body
and mind of Buddha in them. Furthermore, we must *feel* the
'living body-mind of Buddha and the Patriarchs' in them.
Dōgen purposely uses the adjective 'living'. Isn't Dōgen's
own deep religious experience transmitted by it? Certainly
he could perceive the arduous practice of Buddha and the
Patriarchs in each word of the Buddhist scriptures and
teachings, but I think it was something more than that.
Didn't the body-mind of Shakyamuni and the Patriarchs,
who practised with the determination to die if necessary,
fill the mind and body of Dōgen through the scriptures
and spur him on to die the Great Death? And wasn't it
Dōgen's experience 'to verify the Buddha directly for himself
with this body-mind' (*Gakudō Yōjin-shū* [Advice on
Studying the Way])?

Reflecting the mind in an ancient mirror —
a body-mind experience

There is an old saying in Zen, 'Beneath a bright window,
reflect your mind in an ancient mirror.' This means that we
should use the sutras and writings of the Zen Patriarchs as a
bright mirror to shed light on our own minds and examine
whether what we have realized in enlightenment agrees with
them or not. Both must be clear and match each other
exactly. But we should not take this reflecting of the mind
as an internal occurrence. I think we can say with certainty,

at least as far as can be judged from the above words, that Dōgen Zenji understood it as a body-mind event. To reflect the mind in an ancient mirror is an experience of the whole 'body-as-subject' which is made up of body and soul. The 'bodies' of the Buddha and Patriarchs who have practised so arduously take hold of the 'body' of the disciple and practise with him, finally leading him to enlightenment. Then it is verified for the first time that the true enlightenment of the 'bodies' of the Buddha and Patriarchs is identical with the true enlightenment of the 'body' of the Zen disciple. When this happens we can say for the first time that 'each and every line is the living body-mind of the Buddha and Patriarchs'.

This is not merely something that has occurred to me. The words of Dōgen quoted above were spoken in the following context:

> It is good to reflect quietly. This life is short, but if we learn even two or three phrases of the Buddha and Patriarchs, what these words and phrases manifest is the Buddha and Patriarchs themselves. Therefore to truly learn even two or three phrases is to truly experience with your body the Buddha and Patriarchs themselves, for the body-mind of the Buddha and Patriarchs is one, and every phrase they have uttered is the very body-mind in which their warm blood flows. Accordingly, if you study these words and phrases with your whole body and mind, the body-mind of the Buddha and Patriarchs will come and take possession of your own body-mind. Then, precisely at that instant, the accomplishment of the Way of the Buddha and Patriarchs will come and manifest your own body-mind in the accomplishment of the Buddha-way (*Shōbōgenzō*, 'Gyōjika' [Sustained Practice]).

Now, what does Dōgen's reading of the Buddhist scriptures teach Christians about how to read the Bible? Essentially, the Gospels are a record of the words and acts of Jesus. Before I started practising Zen, I read them with my head and heart, trying to know what these words and actions of Jesus were teaching me. I was primarily concerned, therefore, with Christ's teachings and doctrine and finding the way of life that I should imitate.

What I was looking for in the Bible was the teaching of truth that would shed light on my reason and for the example of Christ that would appeal to my heart. This way of reading

Scripture may be beneficial, but it does not clarify the Bible's deeper meaning. When I started to practise Zen and came to understand the words of Dōgen mentioned above, my method of reading the Bible changed completely.

'This is my body'

Following his birth in a stable in Bethlehem, Jesus lived a life of poverty in Nazareth, practised asceticism in the desert for forty days, and led a missionary life of which he could say, 'Foxes have holes, and birds of the air have nests; but the Son of man has nowhere to lay his head' (Matthew 8:20). Finally he died on the cross.

His life could be called a way of suffering, drenched in sweat and blood. To read the Bible is to follow this life of Jesus, but 'to follow' does not mean to picture to yourself the figure of Christ 2,000 years ago, reflecting on the meaning of his words and actions, and trying to regulate your own life after his example. To follow Christ's life you must put your body and soul into walking with Christ and have the 'living body-mind' of the suffering Christ press upon you, urging your whole 'body' towards the same way of suffering, until at last you realize that the 'living body-mind' of Christ is living in your 'body'. Then for the first time you will be able to say, as Paul did, 'Now, not I, but Christ lives in me'. This is how I learned to read the Bible with my whole 'body'.

Actually, this kind of reading of the Bible has been carried out in the Catholic Church since the time of the early Fathers. One of the best examples of it is in the event of the Last Supper as recorded in Matthew 26 and Luke 22. In Matthew's account we read the following: 'Now as they were eating, Jesus took bread, and blessed, and broke it, and gave it to the disciples and said, "Take, eat; this is my body" ' (Matthew 26:26). Some Protestants interpret these words in a spiritual-istic sense, understanding Christ to be spiritually present in the bread when the minister performs the Communion service in accordance with Christ's command. Catholics, however, have taken these words of Christ literally since the beginning of the Church, understanding that when the priest celebrates Mass in obedience to Christ's injunction, the bread becomes the 'living body-mind' of Christ. St Paul declared this explicitly (1 Corinthians 11:23 ff.).

Following this Catholic tradition, we receive the Sacred Body at Mass and firmly believe that at that moment the 'body' of Christ becomes one with our 'bodies'.

From this we can see that the way of reading the Bible I learned from Zen is in accord with Catholic tradition. It is strange that it has not been found up to now in Christianity, as it has developed in the West. I hope in the future to develop this method of reading the Bible with the whole body and mind and create a new kind of scriptural hermeneutics. From what has been said above, it should be clear that this kind of hermeneutics is deeply rooted in Christian tradition.

Love your enemies

I would like to present a concrete example of this sort of scriptural hermeneutics to give the reader an idea of what it is:

> But love your enemies, and do good, and lend, expecting nothing in return; and your reward will be great, and you will be sons of the Most High; for he is kind to the ungrateful and the selfish. Be merciful, even as your Father is merciful (Luke 6:35-36).

This passage is ordinarily interpreted as an exhortation of Christ to us. It is explained that what is being taught is the precept of love of one's enemies which finds its basis in the love of God the Father. This is not an erroneous interpretation, but it seems to me that it considers only the superficial meaning of the words. Its weakness lies in the fact that it cuts off these words from the 'living body-mind' of Christ. As a result, Christ's injunction is reduced to a teaching in which no blood circulates, and it becomes a heavy stone weighing down the hearts of Christians. These are words that came from the mouth of Christ; they are not merely an expression of his Spirit. Shouldn't this passage be understood as the 'living body-mind' of Christ?

The figure of Jesus depicted in the Gospels is literally the figure of a person who 'loves his enemies'. He called Judas, the disciple who betrayed him, 'dear friend', and washed his feet at the Last Supper, making every effort until the very end to bring about a change of heart in him. And when, having been condemned to death, he was nailed to the cross and ridiculed, he prayed for those who reviled him, saying, 'Father, forgive them; for they know not what they do' (Luke 23:34). This is truly the figure of a person who loves his enemies.

I would not interpret this passage by seeing the figure of Christ who 'loves his enemies' in it and resolving to act in accordance with his example, for then the 'body' of Christ would merely become something that existed 2,000 years ago and appeals to me from afar. That kind of interpretation divides the 'body' of Christ and my 'body' into two and puts them in dualistic opposition. Someone with a deep Zen experience would most probably consider a person holding such concepts an incomplete Christian.

Don't I fail to be a true Christian unless the 'living body-mind' of Christ, who loves his enemies to the extent of giving up his life for them, takes hold of my 'body' and urges it towards the way of loving my enemies, finally bringing it to warm life and to a love of my enemies? Then my 'body' is alive but it is not my flesh that lives. I must realize that Christ's 'living body-mind' truly lives in me. Then for the first time I will be able to say that the passage above is not a precept of love but the 'living body-mind' of Christ. Of course, as was explained before, in order to do this one must do zazen with the resolve to die the Great Death and, completely forgetting one's self, become the sacred passage itself.

Learning from Nichiren's 'body-reading'

Thus far I have been saying that the real way to read Scripture and koans is with the 'body', but when you really think about it, shouldn't all religious writings, especially the canons of the world's great religions, be read with the 'body'? Actually, I think it can be said that the great religious teachers and saints, without exception, have done so. Among them, one who was not only aware of the necessity of reading with the 'body' and did so himself, but also made it the core of his teaching to his disciples, was the Buddhist saint Nichiren. This is indicated very concisely in a short letter he wrote that is famous under the title 'The Dungeon Letter'. At the time that Nichiren was about to be banished to the island of Sado, a number of his disciples were also arrested and locked up in a dungeon. Among them was his leading disciple Nichirō. It was to him that the following letter was sent:

> Tomorrow I will leave for Sado. I think with pity of you in the dungeon on this cold night. Honorable Nichirō, if you are a person who realizes even a part of the Lotus Sutra with both body and mind, you will be able to save your family, relatives, and all sentient beings. When others read the Lotus Sutra, they mouth the words, but don't read with the mind. And if they read with the mind, they don't read with the body. To read with both body and mind is the most exalted. It is written, 'Angels will come and serve those who believe in the Lotus Sutra, and though Dharma enemies may try to hurt them with knives or sticks or poison, they will never be able to do so', and so nothing terrible will happen to us. When you get out of prison please come to me immediately. I want to see you, as much as you do me.
>
> Humbly yours,
> Nichiren (seal)

Eighth Year of Bun'ei (1271)
9 October
To Chikugo Dono

This letter overflows with the saint's deep feeling for his favourite disciple. Since Nichiren himself probably had to spend the cold winter nights in a freezing cell, he could sympathize with the shivering body of his disciple. Like himself, the latter was being persecuted for teaching the Lotus Sutra and was enduring the intense cold in prison. Of course, the warm-hearted Nichiren was expressing his genuine feelings in this letter, but it was more than that. He was awakening his beloved disciple to the religious consciousness called 'body-reading' and explaining it in detail to him. According to the Lotus Sutra, those who devote themselves to its recitation will invariably be persecuted, but they will never suffer injury as a result of it. Therefore, in order really to read the sutra it is not enough to simply say the words and understand and believe them in one's heart. Really to read the Lotus Sutra is to 'body-read' it. One must bodily experience religious persecution and realize that one is not harmed by it. One must personally master the way of the true Dharma of the Lotus Sutra and, at the same time, by this means to come to a firm belief that one is a chosen devotee of the Lotus Sutra who has been given the mission to save all sentient beings. This is the 'body-reading' Nichiren is explaining so intimately in this letter.

Every time I read Saint Nichiren's letter I am deeply moved. It forces me to examine my lukewarm way of life as a Christian and my shallow reading of the Bible. After he had prophesied his cross, Jesus taught his disciples to follow the same way: 'If any man would come after me, let him deny himself and take up his cross and follow me' (Matthew 16:24).

Do I, as a Christian, really read these words of Jesus as Nichiren 'body-read' the Lotus Sutra? The 'Dungeon Letter' always brings me to this kind of reflection and constantly teaches me the necessity of 'body-reading' the Bible.

Chapter 14

Towards a new Scriptural hermeneutics

Your body is a temple of the Holy Spirit
(1 Corinthians 6:19)

Towards a new Scriptural hermeneutics

The most important thing I have learned from Zen is how to read the Bible at a deeper level. I mentioned earlier that, for some reason, as I devoted myself to the practice of Zen and passed various koans, I became able to read Scripture more profoundly with the solving of each koan. Or perhaps I should say that the Bible disclosed its deeper meaning to me. Zen practice is very severe and a number of friends have sympathized with me, saying that it must be very hard. But no matter how rigorous and painful a *sesshin* may be, for me it is always a joy to participate in one. When I return from a *sesshin* my Christian prayer improves and I am filled with a sense of the purpose of my religious life. But what is most important, the Bible reveals its deeper significance. It is because of this precious experience that the difficulties of making a *sesshin* seem insignificant to me.

As the Bible has come to open up new dimensions of meaning in this manner, a new way of spiritually reading it has been taking form in me. It might be called a new Scriptural hermeneutics, essentially different from that which has existed up to now. In this chapter I would like to reflect on my own experience and attempt to explain why doing zazen and working on koans has resulted in the creation of this new kind of hermeneutics. In order to do that, however, it is necessary first to describe the psychological make-up involved in solving koans.

It goes without saying that koans cannot be separated from zazen and the direction of a master. If one interprets koans without doing zazen or appearing before the master in *dokusan*, the chances are that in eight or nine cases out of ten, such interpretations will be empty theory or of no real use. Properly speaking, koans form only one part of the Master's training of the disciple and it is taken for granted that they will be worked on through zazen and *dokusan*.

Koans are problems which a Zen master gives a disciple to bring him to enlightenment or, in the case of one who has already attained enlightenment, to cultivate a higher state of realization. The primary goal of a koan is the radical turn-about of the disciple, a complete conversion of his whole personality. This has already been discussed in detail in the section on purification. The second goal of a koan is to bring a person to make the leap from the sphere of discursive thought to that of 'unthought thought'. Koans cannot be solved by the ordinary working of reason. Not until one stills such activity through zazen and attains a higher *prajñā* wisdom can one understand a koan. At first, therefore, it appears to be an enigma. The Zen practitioner who has this riddle thrust before him must get rid of his passions, stop the ordinary working of his reason, and die to himself. From this point of view, koans play the role of a killing sword. Because they were originally expressions of the Zen experience of the early masters, however, to one who has achieved *prajñā* wisdom, koans are expressions of plain truths, and the solution to a koan flows forth naturally and simultaneously from this recognition. Then when the disciple's understanding is approved by the master in *dokusan*, it becomes a *koan* (a public document or case) which certifies the genuineness of the disciple's experience. The koan was originally 'the Zen mirror by which one compares the true nature of saints and ordinary men' (*Chūhō Kōroku* [Records of Chūhō]). Thus the disciple can know that his understanding is 'not the idea of a single person . . . but innately the same supreme principle that has been held by the great masters of all times and places' (*ibid*).

The similar character of koans and the Bible

Scripture and koans are structurally similar in several respects. First of all, the Bible (New Testament) is the message by which Christ the teacher brought his listeners to become his disciples and walk the same path that he did. This is similar to the problem that the Zen master gives his disciple with a koan. Second, Christ's words 'The Kingdom of God is at hand, repent' (Mark 1:15) are a demand for an existential conversion. This corresponds to the role of a koan as a turning question (i.e., one which turns man's delusion to enlightenment). Third, just as a koan manifests the level of the 'unthought thought', the message that the Bible gives us about God is always only a 'pointing toward an incomprehensible mystery'. Fourth, corresponding to Bultman's observation that the message of the Bible leads man to self-comprehension, koans are for the purpose of looking into one's self and for leading to a realization of the Original Self. And finally, in the same way that koans cannot be separated from zazen and *dokusan*, the Catholic Church has insisted from the beginning that meditation, spiritual direction, and the guidance of the Church are necessary for a proper interpretation of the Bible.

It is not at all surprising, therefore, that I should have learned a new Scriptural hermeneutics from Zen. Scripture and koans are quite different in terms of content, but because they resemble each other in the five respects mentioned above, it is not only possible to apply the method of solving koans to the interpretation of the Bible, I think it can even be called the best way. Christians have traditionally come to realize the deeper import of Scripture by meditating on it. If, as I said above, we realize that the prayer of the 'body' by means of zazen surpasses the kind of meditation we have done up to now, and if we were to adopt zazen instead of it, a superior Scriptural hermeneutics would be created as a natural consequence. As I mentioned before, the message of the Bible explains divine mysteries and cannot be understood through the ordinary working of reason. But because grappling with koans through the practice of zazen and going to *dokusan* brings a person to a higher wisdom that transcends reason, it is an excellent way to unravel the mysteries of the Bible. From the beginning the Church has, in fact, attached great importance to wisdom (Greek *sophia*, Latin *sapientia*) and has firmly held that things pertaining to God and the message of the Bible can be truly understood only by means of it. It is a higher wisdom which transcends reason and is bestowed on man by God.

Let me explain this new way of reading Scripture more concretely. I mentioned earlier that when I return from a *sesshin* the Bible discloses its deeper significance to me. It was from this personal experience that the idea for a new way of reading Scripture came. When I do zazen, I sit in single-minded concentration. Now if I maintain that state of *samādhi* and read a line or passage of Scripture and then pause quietly, letting myself sink into deep contemplation, the profound meaning of the sacred words wells up within me. This is truly an exhilarating experience. It might be compared to the experience of a person who roars with laughter when he suddenly sees through a Zen koan.

As a matter of fact, this way of reading Scripture is exactly the same as that used in solving a koan. You ponder a koan after you have completely entered *samādhi*. If your mind is not unified and concentrated, no matter how much you grapple with it, you will not be able to solve it. Or, I should say, thinking discursively about the koan only results in disturbing your *samādhi*. You cannot really ponder a koan until you are at the point where your state of *samādhi* remains undisturbed even though you bring the koan to mind. For that reason you have to study the koan well before doing zazen and commit its essential points to memory. In the same way, of course, when you want to meditate on a passage of the Bible, it is important to first go over it thoroughly. If you then enter *samādhi* by doing zazen and reach the point where your mind is undisturbed even when the passage is introduced, and if you can remain in that state, you will, so to speak, be able to become one with the passage.

Since changing to this way of reading the Bible, I have become increasingly aware that each passage holds a meaning more profound than I had ever imagined.

Our bodies are the home of the Holy Spirit

For now, I would like to choose just one of the Scriptural
passages I have read in this way and try to explain it. It is a
sentence from St Paul: 'Your body is a temple of the Holy
Spirit' (1 Corinthians 6:19). The word 'body' is used many
times in the Bible to indicate the whole person. The Bible
does not separate the body from the soul as the Greeks did,
nor does it hold that the soul is noble and the body base. In
Scripture as these words of Paul indicate so well, the body
manifests man's sanctity. Up to now many Christians have
interpreted these words in a spiritualistic sense, thinking that
God lives in the soul or heart of a person and that the body
is only an outer covering. In the Bible, however, 'body'
refers to the whole person as a living body and is very close
in meaning to the 'body' described above in phenomenological terms. Divine grace is given not only to the soul, but
to the 'body' of the whole person. Furthermore, it is not
only divine grace, according to Paul, but God Himself who
lives in the 'body'. The theological basis for the complete
purification of the body that I discussed in a previous chapter
lies in this thought of Paul. (And since Paul's idea originated
in the words of Christ, we can ultimately call it the thought
of Christ.) The Holy Spirit, the Spirit of God, spiritualizes all
creation and divinizes man. Paul says that this Holy Spirit is
within us and prays to God the Father, crying, 'Abba, Father'.
Therefore the fact that man's 'body' is 'a temple of the Holy
Spirit' has profound meaning: Christian prayer is not man
addressing God but God, the Holy Spirit, speaking to God,
the Father, and we are one with this act.

Notice that in this quotation Paul says decisively, 'Your
body is a temple of the Holy Spirit.' He does not command
us, 'Be a temple of the Holy Spirit.' Whether or not we are
conscious of it, the 'body' of a Christian is existentially 'a
temple of the Holy Spirit'. Paul is pointing out the strict
reality. This reality is deeply buried in us, however, side by
side with the root of original sin. Thus it is usually forgotten
or ignored and there are few persons who grasp it with their
whole 'body'.

What is necessary in order to become aware of this hidden

reality? Two things are required. The first is to eradicate the root of original sin and the second is to dig up what has been deeply buried. The first step is purification or emancipation and the second is the awakening of *prajñā* wisdom (called *sophia* or *sapientia* in Christianity, as I mentioned earlier). In the first part of this book I explained how complete purification can be accomplished through doing zazen and working on koans, so that it is hardly necessary to explain again that doing zazen is an excellent way to attain *prajñā* wisdom. From my own limited experience, I can say that by doing zazen it is possible to easily awaken to the reality that 'Your body is a temple of the Holy Spirit'. Let me explain why.

When the 'body' has been purified through composure of body, breath and mind, the living 'temple of the Holy Spirit' becomes activated. The Holy Spirit begins to move of himself, quieting the fires of passion, eradicating the root of original sin, and making the 'body' into a fitting home for himself. The 'temple of the Holy Spirit' has awakened from a deep sleep; *sapientia* is set in motion and a person comes to realize that he is 'a temple of the Holy Spirit'. This realization is a kind of spiritual awakening and not the reflective functioning of reason. It might be better called 'active intuition', to borrow a term from Nishida philosophy, which is executed by the whole 'body'. By becoming one with the Holy Spirit and His functioning within the 'body', we intuit directly at the centre of that very activity.

Try to imagine a Christian who, moved by an interior compulsion devotes himself to the practice of zazen. After several months of arduous practice, he suddenly awakens one day to the marvellous reality of Paul's words, 'Your body is a temple of the Holy Spirit.' He realizes that prayer is not himself speaking to God with human words, but God speaking within him in His own words. When his whole 'body' is penetrated by and made one with this reality, and he realizes that this is rightly his own prayer, that it comes from his own heart, and that this is what real prayer is, how great his joy will be!

Part III

The *Spiritual Exercises* and a Zen *sesshin*

Chapter 15

To die the Great Death and be born again

Step forward from the top of a 100-foot pole

If a grain of wheat dies it bears much fruit
(John 12:24)

The conception of the Spiritual Exercises

It is common for members of Catholic religious orders to make a full eight-day retreat each year and once or twice in their lifetime to participate in a month-long retreat. The latter is a religious discipline based on Ignatius of Loyola's *Spiritual Exercises*. This work was originally a draft made by Ignatius on the basis of his personal religious experience. In the course of using it to direct others, he found it necessary to revise and supplement it, and finally it was brought together into one volume. To help the reader understand the *Exercises*, I would like to give a short biography of Ignatius and sketch the historical background of the book.

Ignatius was born in 1491, the youngest son of the noble family of Loyola, in the Spanish Basque country. (The Loyola castle still stands there.) When Ignatius grew up, he served the king of Castile as an outstanding knight. Besides becoming accomplished in the martial arts, he developed a chivalrous spirit and matured in character. At the same time, however, Ignatius was addicted to gambling and romantic affairs with women. When he was thirty years old, he was involved in a skirmish at Pamplona where his troops were attacked by the numerically superior French. The tide of the battle turned against them and all were about to surrender, but Ignatius fighting with great bravery and determination, persuaded the lord of the castle to continue the battle. Several days later, however, he was wounded in the leg by an enemy shell and the castle finally surrendered. The French troops were so impressed by his knightly valour that they escorted the wounded Ignatius back to Loyola castle. To overcome his boredom during the long period of recuperation, Ignatius read the *Life of Christ* and a collection of the lives of the saints and was converted as a result. Going to Manresa in Spain, he secluded himself in an isolated cave where he abstained from meat and began a life of begging for alms. Every day he would kneel in prayer for six or seven hours. In time, by the grace of God, he had a number of deep mystical experiences, which he recorded in a notebook. Later these notes were brought together into a small book called the *Spiritual Exercises*. Among the spiritual experiences Ignatius received from God, the interior illumination he had on the banks of the Cardoner River is famous. In his later years he was to speak about this experience as follows:

> Once I went to St Paul's Church about 1.5 kilometers from Manresa. The road ran along a river. As I walked, I was immersed in devout thoughts and at one point sat down for a while facing the downward flow of the river. As I was sitting there my eyes of intellect began to open. But what I saw was not an apparition; I was able to understand many spiritual matters related to both faith and learning. I was so brightly illumined by this that everything seemed to be new.
>
> I realized so many things at this time that it is impossible to give a detailed explanation of them all. But it is certain that my reason was greatly illumined. I think that if all the things God has taught me during my 62 years of life and everything I have learned on my own were put into one, it still would not come near to the illumination of that moment. (Author's translation.)

This experience can be called a kind of enlightenment. Notice that according to the account he did not see an object; it was 'not an apparition'. This opening of the 'eyes of intellect' (*los ojos del entendimiento*) was an absolutely new kind of illumination.

Later Ignatius was to use this experience at Manresa and the rough draft of the *Exercises* to direct others. While studying in Paris he began to live a religious life with seven comrades. He expanded this group and later founded the Society of Jesus which was to bring about a great reform in the history of the Catholic Church.

Eradicating self-love — the first similarity

As might be surmised from this background sketch, Ignatius's lofty spirit of chivalry runs through the *Spiritual Exercises*. It is very similar to the austere and all-out spirit found in a Zen *sesshin*. Since I was well acquainted with the spirit of the Exercises, from the first time I took part in a *sesshin* it did not strike me as at all severe, and I even felt a certain familiarity. As we saw in the abridged biography above, the Exercises were born of Ignatius's deep religious experience and are meant to lead the retreatant to the same kind of experience. In this respect they are the same as a Zen *sesshin*. The latter also comes from the religious experience of the Zen masters and has been refined over a long period of time. Through a *sesshin* the Zen practitioner is led to the same kind of religious experience as that of the early Zen masters.

In the beginning of the *Spiritual Exercises* it says: 'Just as strolling, walking and running are bodily exercises, so spiritual exercises are methods of preparing and disposing the soul' (Exercise 1). They are called spiritual exercises because they involve self-examination, meditation, attendance at Mass, morning and evening prayers, spiritual direction (corresponding to *dokusan* in Zen), manual work, and religious austerities. Ignatius does not stipulate in detail regarding bodily posture during prayer and meditation but says, 'At times kneeling, at times prostrate on the ground, at other times supine, or seated or standing, always intent on seeking what I desire' (Exercise 76). Therefore adopting the method of zazen presents no difficulty at all. Ignatius also adds two precautions which apply perfectly to zazen. The first is not to change one's posture during a meditation and the second is that 'When I find that which I desire, I will meditate quietly, without being anxious to continue further until I have satisfied myself' (*Ibid.*). There is no better posture for remaining motionless and steady, and no more excellent way of fixing the mind on one point, than that of zazen. I explained before why zazen can make a great contribution to Christian prayer, and we can see here how it also suits the prescriptions of the Ignatian Exercises.

Ignatius demands the following attitude of a person who is about to begin the Exercises: he must offer up his entire will and freedom and begin the Exercises with a spirit of great courage and generosity. Not permitting this attitude to end in mere spiritualism, Ignatius asks that it be put into practice concretely during the Exercises by carefully observing the time allotted for the Exercises and faithfully carrying out their detailed prescriptions. For example, he says that each of the five hours of daily meditation should be a full hour and that rather than less, it is better to spend more time in meditation. Ignatius observes that it is especially hard to pray for an hour when one feels tired or desolate, but he stipulates that 'to fight against desolation and to conquer temptation, the exercitant should continue a little beyond the full hour' (Exercise 13). This prescription is called turning in the opposite direction (*agere contra*) and it is recommended that the retreatant carry it out whenever he finds himself in an adverse situation. For example, 'If such a soul has any inordinate inclinations or attachments, it will be most useful for it to work as forcefully as possible to attain the contrary of that to which the present attachment tends' (Exercise 16). If these instructions, prescriptions, and attitudes were to be applied, just as they are, to Zen practice, they would not be in the least bit incongruous. Let me point out two or three analogous passages from Dōgen Zenji's writings.

> One must be careful in studying the Way, to get rid of one's main attachment.

> First faithfully observe the practice of the precepts, subduing the mind and reforming oneself.

Citing the arduous practice of the Patriarchs, he says:

> The men of old cut off their arms and fingers. . . . In ancient times Buddha left his home and renounced his country. . . . Know that a person who seeks an easy way will never be enlightened.

An old master once said, 'You must step forward from the top of a 100-ft pole.' This means you must cast off both mind and body, as if you had climbed to the top of a 100-ft pole and let go with both your hands and feet.

Ignatius teaches the same kind of complete renunciation: 'Reflect on the fact that one will advance in all spiritual matters in proportion to the degree that one gets rid of self-love, self-will and egoism' (Exercise 189). Thus we see that the first point of resemblance between the *Spiritual Exercises* and a Zen *sesshin* is the great courage and spirit of renunciation demanded at the beginning of the Exercises.

Retreat and silence — the second similarity

The second point of similarity between the two is the going into retirement for a time and keeping silent. A Zen *sesshin* is usually held at a Zen *dōjō* in a secluded wooded area. The monk practitioners confine themselves to the innermost Zen hall of the temple for seven days and, cutting off all communication with the outside world, devote themselves to zazen. Silence is strictly observed and the mind is quieted interiorly as well. A Catholic retreat is also conducted at a secluded monastery or retreat house and all contact with the outside world suspended. Everything, including eating and manual labour, is done in silence; the retreatant separates himself from all things exterior and interior and devotes himself to prayer. Ignatius comments,

Being thus separated, not having his mind divided by many things but *giving all his care to only one*, which is the service of his Creator and the profiting of his own soul, he is more at liberty to use his natural ability in searching more diligently for what he desires so strongly' (Exercise 20; italics mine). (Author's translation.)

What should be noted in particular in this passage is the fact that serving God and one's own salvation are not interpreted dualistically. Proof of this is that if they were separated the retreatant would not be concentrating on only one thing, and the instruction to give 'all his care to only one' would be a contradiction. In Buddhist terminology, these two are in the relationship of 'not the same and not separate'.

The Great Death-Great Life dynamism — the third similarity

The third point of resemblance between a *sesshin* and a retreat is the dynamic life principle of the Great Death and Great Life. The famous Zen words 'To die the Great Death and be born again' express this dynamism very well. Needless to say, a *sesshin* is permeated with this principle from beginning to end. Similar words can also be found in Catholic spiritual teaching.

> Unless a grain of wheat falls into the earth and dies, it remains alone; but if it dies, it bears much fruit. He who loves his life loses it, and he who hates his life in this world will keep it for eternal life (John 12:24-25).

This life principle also operates in the whole of the Exercises. Let us look at how it does so in the concrete by examining each of the four weeks of the Exercises.

The first week of the Exercises

The main goal of the first week of the Exercises is conversion. The foremost problem, therefore, is conversion from sin, which is demanded so that one may live the life of God. Thus the theme of the first week is to come to life by dying to sin. As I mentioned earlier when discussing purification in Zen and Christianity, Christian purification and Zen emancipation are very similar. The situation does not differ in the first week of the Exercises. Because the theme of the first week is meditation on sin, it differs from a Zen *sesshin* in this respect, but if we examine it closely, we find that there is something in Zen which corresponds to the first week of the Exercises, as the following words of Master Shōsan Suzuki indicate:

> There is a principle one should take care to know after receiving tonsure and the precepts. This body is filthy and defiled, a body of evil passions. It is an ignorant and dull body, a body which should descend to the four evil worlds (i.e., hell, the world of hungry

spirits, the world of animals, and the world of fighting demons). Yet the Buddhas and Patriarchs came into this world and, by the merits of their arduous practice, gave us manifold expedient means and left us an infinite variety of teachings. How grateful we are for the power of their vow to save all beings which has come down to us in this last generation of the corrupt world. . . . Joy of joys, there is nothing greater than to become a Buddhist disciple. You must make a holy vow to be emancipated from delusive passions and attain Buddhahood without fail and to observe the teachings of the Buddhas and Patriarchs (*Rokusō-bun* [Parting Grasses at the Foot of the Mountain]).

These sentences are set against a background of Buddhist thought, but there are passages in the Exercises which, although they have a Christian nuance, resemble them:

Let me consider all my own corruption and foulness of body. Let me see myself as a sore and an abscess from whence have come forth so many sins, so many evils, and the most vile poison (Exercise 58).

How often I have deserved to be damned externally for the many sins I have committed (Exercise 48).

Imagine Christ our Lord before you, hanging on the cross. . . . I will end this meditation with a colloquy directing my thoughts to God's mercy. I will give thanks to Him for having granted me life until now, and I will resolve with the help of His grace to amend my life for the future (Exercise 61).

I must reflect deeply on myself and ask, 'What have I done for Christ? What am I doing now for Christ? What ought I to do for Christ?' (Exercise 53).

In these words, as in those of Master Shōsan Suzuki quoted above, we can find the following concepts: a body defiled by sinful acts, salvation through the merits of the ascetic practice of the religious founders, one's gratitude and joy for it, and a resolution for the future.

From this consideration it should be clear, I think, how greatly the first week of the *Spiritual Exercises* resembles a Zen *sesshin*.

Chapter 16

With a distinguished spirit of chivalry

'The Kingdom of Christ' (*Spiritual Exercises*,
Second Week)

The sustained practice of the Buddhas and
Patriarchs (Dōgen)

The second week of the Spiritual Exercises

In the previous chapter I described the third similarity between the *Spiritual Exercises* and a Zen *sesshin* — the principle of the Great Death and Great Life. We saw that the dynamism of a *sesshin*, 'To die the Great Death and be reborn', also runs through a Catholic retreat. Having completed the explanation of how this point of resemblance was found in the first week of the Exercises, I would like to continue our inquiry now starting from the second week.

The task set for the retreatant at the beginning of the second week of the Exercises is the important contemplation called 'The Kingdom of Christ'. This is the main practice dominating the second week. The Great Death-Great Life principle is also pulsating here, but it appears under a form so different from that of the first week that at first glance it may not seem to be operative. The central theme of the first week was dying to sin, which thrust the Great Death to the forefront and made it easy to see the Great Life as its reverse side. In 'The Kingdom of Christ', however, the problem is how the retreatant will respond to Christ's invitation. Desiring the salvation of all men, Christ gathers his disciples and tells them that he wants them to work with him towards this goal. 'How will you as Christ's disciple respond to this ardent desire?' This is the fundamental point of contemplation of 'The Kingdom of Christ'.

It is not easy to see the Great Death-Great Life here. Furthermore, the content is so Christian and so completely foreign to Zen that it seems hard to find any point of resemblance with a *sesshin*. As a matter of fact, a number of Christian theologians have proposed that the thought underlying 'The Kingdom of Christ' is the fundamental difference between Zen and Christianity. Even priests with a fair amount of actual experience in the practice of Zen have held this, and some still do. I myself used to think this way. Recently, however, I have become aware of a great resemblance between them which I would like to talk about more in this chapter. But first let us look at a synopsis of the contemplation on 'The Kingdom of Christ'.

By the second week of the Exercises, the retreatant has already been purified and we can say that, to a certain extent, he has died the Great Death and been born again to the Great Life. In the final meditation of the first week, the retreatant pictures before him Christ nailed to the cross and, recalling that he underwent such a cruel death for our sins, reflects deeply on what he himself must do for this Christ. If a person does this on the visceral level, in his *hara*, he will cry out as Paul did at the moment of his conversion outside Damascus, 'What am I to do, Lord?' (Acts 22:10). Only the retreatant who is on this level can enter contemplation of 'The Kingdom of Christ'. To the person who has this kind of attitude, Christ beckons, saying, 'It is my will to conquer the whole world and all my enemies, and thus to enter into the glory of my Father. Whoever wishes to come with me must labour with me, so that following me in suffering, he may also follow me in glory' (Exercise 95). The person who has a distinguished spirit of chivalry, good judgment, and a sincere heart will respond to Christ's invitation and devote himself completely to this undertaking. But he will not only offer his body. Conquering his fleshly tendencies and worldly loves, he will make an even more precious and important offering. This is how Ignatius describes it in the Exercises.

The Ignatian spirit of chivalry

This is a summary of 'The Kingdom of Christ' which, as we can see, is overflowing with the author's spirit of chivalry. The faithful servant Ignatius ardently desires to make a greater offering than anyone else to his Lord Christ. His love for Christ prompts him not only to fight against his encumbering desires, but directs him towards even greater self-sacrifice. The dynamism of the Great Death-Great Life is pulsating here in a hidden form. To be brought to life by Christ's love is the Great Life, but it signifies an even greater death. To put it more precisely, the love of Christ is witnessed to only by the Great Death of self-oblation. Only where there is the Great Death (self-oblation) is the Great Life (love of Christ) revealed. The Great Life does not follow the Great Death, however; self-oblation itself is the love of Christ. The Great Death is the Great Life. To take it a step further, we can say that at the same time that the love of Christ is the love of the retreatant for Christ, it is also Christ's love for the retreatant. The former does not exist until it is brought to life and put in motion by the latter. The retreatant's love is Christ's love.

Now, in what respect does the meditation on 'The Kingdom of Christ' resemble a *sesshin*? The former puts so much stress on Christian love and a personal relationship with Christ that the reader may wonder how it could have anything in common with the latter. But there is a point of resemblance and it is found, surprisingly, in the private encounter with the Zen master in *dokusan*. Let me tell you how I came to discover this resemblance.

Before I began to practise Zen, I thought, like most people, that the distinctive characteristic of Christianity was a personal relationship and that this was not found in Zen or, at least, that it was not an important part of Zen. But after I started doing Zen seriously, I gradually became aware that the relation between a Zen master and his disciple is a personal relationship in the best sense of the word. Actually, from ancient times 'seeing eye to eye with the master' has been highly valued in Zen. The master under whom I am practising is always telling us that when you encounter a master whom you feel is the true one for you, you should 'devote yourself to him so completely that you would not hesitate to offer up your life for him' and follow that master to the end, and that this is of the essence in Zen practice. Doesn't this resemble the Christian who follows 'only one Master', Christ, to the very end? My experience in Zen has taught me that they are structurally the same. If then, granting this, we can say that Christ has a personal relationship with his disciples, why can't we call the relationship of a Zen master with his disciples a personal one?

Here, in order to avoid any misunderstanding, I should also touch on the differences between the two. The meditation on 'The Kingdom of Christ' presupposes a belief in the God-man Christ, so that in a certain respect the relationship between Christ and his disciples and that of a Zen master and his disciples is different. The former is a relationship between the God-man and men whereas the latter is a relationship between men. In Zen, the disciple respects the master as his teacher, but in their man-to-man relations they are equal. Furthermore, when the disciple has a great enlightenment, master and disciple, just as they are, are both Buddhas and equal. The relation between Christ and his disciple, on the contrary, has the dual structure of God-to-man and man-to-man. Between God and man there is the superior-subordinate relationship of Creator and creature. But I think it is possible to say that the relation of Christ as man to his disciples is the same as that in Zen.

As I began to notice that there was a personal relationship in Zen, my eyes were also gradually being opened to the similar nature of koans and Scripture. About that time, I was fortunate enough to have the opportunity to read Professor Kanshō Ueda's *Zen Bukkyō* (Zen Buddhism, Chikuma Publishers, Tokyo, 1973) which threw great light on this problem and enabled me to find points of resemblance in 'The Kingdom of Christ' and the practice of Zen.

Meeting the master in dokusan — a person-to-person encounter

Appearing before the Zen master in a private interview called *dokusan* is a concrete unfolding of the personal relationship between master and disciple. The topic taken up in this interview is a Zen dialogue or *mondō* (literally, question and answer), but it is fundamentally different from the Western style of colloquy found in Plato's *Dialogues*. The subject of the latter is objective truth as perceived by reason, which can be read and understood by a third person not on the scene. In such a case, not only is a direct person-to-person confrontation unnecessary, but you do not even need the asking and answering of questions.

A Zen *mondō*, however, cannot materialize without a direct confrontation of two persons; it does not come into being until there is the activity of asking and answering questions. The 'truth' that is the subject of the dialogue cannot be grasped intellectually, however. It is an 'objective truth' realized through a dynamic interpersonal relationship, a reality formed by what Rinzai Zenji calls the 'vital functioning of the true man'. Therefore, no third-person observer is allowed to be present at a Zen *mondō*. The subject cannot be comprehended until one personally takes part in it. In this sense, Zen 'truth' and Zen *mondō* are extremely personal.

No third-person observers are permitted in the contemplation of 'The Kingdom of Christ' either. Only the person who makes the positive commitment, 'What am I to do, Lord?' can 'participate'. The dialogue between Christ and his disciple is an interchange in which the activity of Christ's questioning and the disciple's replying takes place in a tense and mutually responsive atmosphere. Yet 'The Kingdom of Christ' is not realized merely by this interpersonal activity. It is not truly actualized until the disciple loves Christ to the point of throwing away his life for him. This reflection has, I hope, made it easier to find a structural similarity between a Zen *mondō* and 'The Kingdom of Christ'.

The resemblance does not end here, however. Going a step further, we can say that the point towards which both are ultimately directed is also similar. At the end of the contemplation of 'The Kingdom of Christ', the retreatant consecrates himself to Christ and vows from the bottom of his heart:

> It is my wish and desire, and my deliberate choice, provided only that it be for Thy greater service and praise, to imitate Thee in bearing all injuries, all evils, and all poverty both physical and spiritual, if Thy most Sacred Majesty should will to choose me for such a life and state (Exercise 98).

There is the dynamic throbbing of the Great Death and Great Life in this vow. The resolution 'to imitate Thee' is to become poor with Christ who became poor and to desire humiliation with Christ who was humiliated.

The vow to save all sentient beings and the perpetuation of the Way through sustained practice (Dōgen)

Can we find anything that corresponds to this in the private interview between Zen master and disciple? Clearly such a correspondence does not appear in the wording of the Zen *mondō*. But, in fact, a person who has taken part in such a dialogue will become aware in some way of experiencing the following. When he enters the *dokusan* room, he finds the master afire with the vow to save all beings. When the disciple leaves the room, after having come in contact with the master, the resolution to imitate the master and follow this Way to the finish should well up from the bottom of his *hara*, whether or not he is conscious of it. The deeper this determination, the more surely he will turn in the direction indicated by the Four Vows: 'Sentient beings are numberless, I vow to save them; delusive passions are endless, I vow to cut them off; the Dharma gates are endless, I vow to master them; the Buddha Way is unattainable, I vow to attain it.'

We should take note in particular of the last of the Four Vows because it bears a strong resemblance to the fundamental thought of 'The Kingdom of Christ'. But first, savour the following words of Dōgen Zenji:

> In the Great Way of the Buddhas and Patriarchs there is invariably the supreme practice which is constantly sustained without inter-

ruption. It continues from the first stirring of the desire to follow the Way, through practice, true enlightenment and the attainment of Buddhahood without the slightest break. This is the perpetuation of the Way through sustained practice. . . . The power of this practice sustains myself as well as others. This means that the merit of my continuous practice, just as it is, extends throughout heaven and earth. . . . It is by the sustained practice of all the Buddhas and Patriarchs that our sustained practice is realized and that our Great Way has come into being (*Shōbōgenzō*, 'Gyōji' ['Sustained Practice']).

Dōgen tells us that the Way of Buddha is the perpetuation of the supreme and sustained practice of the Buddhas and Patriarchs, and that it has been maintained even to our present age, actualizing our practice. Furthermore, by our sustained practice, the Great Way of Buddha is communicated to the whole world. It is not difficult to find something similar in Ignatius's teaching of 'The Kingdom of Christ'. The latter originated in the crucifixion and resurrection of Christ. This saving act has generated infinite merit, which extends to the whole world and all mankind, calling us even today to 'The Kingdom of Christ'. When we respond to this invitation with our whole being, 'The Kingdom of Christ' is extended to the whole world.

Chapter 17

The super-logic of the 'fool'

The three modes of humility and the three classes
of men

Jōshū sees through an old woman (*Mumonkan*,
Case 31), and National Teacher Daitō

The psychology of 'The Three Classes of Men' (Exercise 149)

In the previous chapter I explained the contemplation at the
beginning of the second week of the Exercises, 'The Kingdom
of Christ', comparing it with Zen. This meditation is both the
basis of the second week of the Exercises and the driving
force behind it. The retreatant places the fundamental spirit
of 'The Kingdom of Christ' in his *hara* and meditates on
Christ's incarnation, birth and life on earth. Then he is finally
confronted with the central problem of the Exercises:
choosing a way of life. In the case of a retreatant who has not
yet decided his place in society or the occupation that he will
pursue, a way of life must be decided. The retreatant who has
already done so must once again confirm his choice and, in
order to press on with a more indomitable and unswerving
spirit, meditate as one does who is making the choice of a
way of life.

As the time to make this choice comes near, the retreatant
must meditate on three things in particular, and in all these
meditations there are points which greatly concur with the
Zen spirit. It is impossible to cover all three in detail here, so
I would like to limit my explanation to just two of them:
contemplation of 'The Three Classes of Men' and 'The

Three Modes of Humility'. The former was not actually included in the early draft of the *Exercises*, but as Ignatius tried to guide persons by giving them the Exercises, he discovered that many had unforeseen attachments and thus did not make progress along the spiritual way. To help these persons get rid of their hidden attachments, he added the meditation on the three classes of men.

The meditation goes as follows. We have here three classes of men and each man has acquired ten thousand ducats. All three men desire to save their souls and since their attachment to this money is an obstacle to salvation, they wish to free themselves from it. The men of the first class are those who would like to get rid of this attachment, but right up to the hour of death take no means to do so. Men of the second class are those who want to free themselves of the attachment but also keep the money they have acquired. Even though they know that to throw away what they have acquired is a superior way, they make no resolve to do so. Since the men of the first and second classes are weak-willed and not seriously intent on doing religious practice, they present no problem worthy of consideration from either the Christian or Zen points of view. The attitude that Ignatius demands as absolutely necessary for the person choosing a way of life is that of the man of the third class. Here what in Zen is called 'transcending dualistic relativism' shows itself clearly in Christian garb. Ignatius describes the state of men of the third class thus:

> They wish to free themselves of the attachment (*affecto*), but in such a way that their inclination (*affection*) will be neither to retain the thing acquired nor not to retain it, desiring to act only as God our Lord shall inspire them and as it shall seem better for the service and praise of His Divine Majesty (Exercise 155).

Most persons think that because the men of the second class want to keep the acquired money and get rid only of the attachment to it, the more perfect men of the third class free themselves of the attachment by getting rid of the money itself. But this is not the thought of Ignatius. To let go of your acquisitions is still imperfect. If you continue to be caught up by dualistic thinking about whether or not to keep what you have acquired, something is wrong. It is only when you transcend this dualistic way of looking at things that you will have freed yourself of attachment in the true sense of the word. This is the negative side of 'The Three Classes of Men'.

God our Lord – one who has transcended duality

There is a positive side as well, however, which is inseparable from the negative. In the last half of the quotation from Ignatius above it says, 'desiring to act only as God our Lord shall inspire them'. We must be aware here that 'God our Lord' cannot be discerned conceptually. Therefore Ignatius is not presenting an idea of God. In the terminology of Professor Kitaro Nishida, it is a spiritual fact, not a subjective fact created by the imagination of Christians. I think no one who has read the autobiography and diaries of Ignatius could doubt that he was a very dispassionate, level-headed person, but one who had a profound mastery of spiritual reality. If we think of 'God our Lord' as a spiritual reality closely resembling the absolute Mu of Nishida philosophy, it can be more or less easily understood by someone with a Zen experience. This 'God our Lord' is not something that stands in opposition to me; God is not a relative being and therefore cannot be grasped relatively. To say that God is immanently transcendent may be somewhat closer to the truth. Thomas Aquinas says, 'God is immanent in us while containing us.' St Augustine expresses God's nearness with the words, 'God is closer to me than I am to myself.'

What Aquinas and Augustine are trying to signify verbally is the spiritual reality of the immanently transcendant God. God is more profoundly my centre than I am the centre of myself. In that sense, everything that emanates from God comes more deeply from the core of me than anything that originates with myself. The desires and plans that originate in God come more deeply from my core than anything that comes from myself. In this sense, we can say that God's wishes are wishes that come from a self that is more truly me than the one from which my own ordinary desires do.

If we think about it in this way, we can understand the meaning of the words quoted above: 'desiring to act only as God our Lord shall inspire them.' God awakens impulses and desires at my core, yet neither God nor those impulses and desires are relative to me. If I have really abandoned all attachments, then that which is my centre is realized as 'nearer to me than I am to myself'. To rephrase it in Zen terminology, the more I die the Great Death, the more God is 'not the same and not separate' from me and the more God's wishes are my wishes and my wishes God's wishes. (If one has not died the Great Death, however, he is not aware of God's closeness as was just described; he thinks of God as someone far away and falls into dualistic relativism.)

This reflection allows us to conclude that in the spiritual structure of the men of the third class there is something very similar to Zen. What a Zen master emphasizes most in training a disciple is the getting rid of this dualistic outlook. Until the disciple does so, not only will he be unable to attain enlightenment, but he will never achieve the highest state in Zen, the unfettered movement of the *samādhi* of innocent delight as depicted in the tenth of the Ox Harding Pictures, 'Entering the City with Empty Hands.' Unhampered by worries about whether he must save all beings or not, just acting in conformity with the desires of his heart, but with a freedom which is spontaneously in accord with Dharma principles — this is truly the state of the great man of Zen. In it there is not even a shadow of dualistic opposition. This state of realization bears a very close resemblance to that which Ignatius demands of the retreatant in 'The Three Classes of Men'. Is St Augustine not saying the same thing with his words, 'Love and do what you will'? If you become one with God through love, using the words of Ignatius quoted above, you will desire to act only as God our Lord shall inspire you.

'The Three Modes of Humility' (Exercise 167) — the way of the 'fool'

In preparing to choose a way of life, the retreatant must do another important religious practice, 'The Three Modes of Humility'. Ignatius does not call this a contemplation, but expects the retreatant to reflect on it many times during the day. Thus it is not material for contemplation. Rather, like the Zen practitioner who is working on a koan, one should ponder it all through the day.

The first mode of humility is to refuse to 'give considera- tion to the thought of breaking any commandment, divine or human, that binds me under pain or mortal sin, even though this offence would make me master of all creation or would preserve my life on earth (Exercise 165). If we were to seek a correspondence to this in Zen, we would find it in the person who has resolved that no matter how many worldly posses- sions he has accumulated, or though his life should be taken from him, nothing could ever induce him to act contrary to the Buddhist Way or bring disgrace to the Buddhas and Patriarchs. Such a person is certainly worthy of respect, but Ignatius desires more than this of the retreatant. And that is the second mode of humility: 'I am in possession of it if my state of mind is such that I neither desire nor even prefer to have riches rather than poverty, to seek honour rather than dishonour, to have a long life rather than a short one' (Exercise 166).

If to desire poverty or wealth, dishonour or honour, a short life or a long one made no special difference in the attainment of our ultimate goal, how would we decide to act? The ordinary person would choose wealth, honour and a long life over poverty, dishonour and a short life. This would present no obstacle to the Way of God and such a person could be a splendid Christian. Nevertheless Ignatius desires something higher from the retreatant. He demands the state where you 'neither desire nor even prefer to have riches rather than poverty, to seek honour rather than dishonour, to have a long life rather than a short one.' In Zen it would be called the state where one has transcended the dualism of poverty and riches, dishonour and honour, long life and short. Ignatius was well aware of man's propensity towards wealth, honour and a long life and knew what one must do in order to break free of dualistic relativism in regard to them and their opposites. With these words, therefore, he is indicating a concrete plan for doing so.

A person who has reached the second mode of humility can be said to have advanced to a very high level. There would seem to be no more perfect state. However, Ignatius indicates to the retreatant that from his own experience there is a higher level. It is the third mode of humility. So Christian is this way that it may seem to have no parallel in Zen, but a closer investigation shows that actually this is not so.

> The third mode of humility is the most perfect. This exists when, the first and second forms already possessed and the praise and glory of the Divine Majesty being equally served, I desire and choose poverty with Christ poor rather than riches, in order to be more like Christ our Lord. When I choose reproaches with Christ thus suffering rather than honour, and when I am willing to be considered as worthless and a fool for Christ Who suffered such treatment before me, rather than to be esteemed as wise and prudent in this world (Exercise 167).

Now let us suppose here that there are two separate ways: one is to be respected by society as a great scholar and the other is to be despised by men as a fool. No matter which way a person takes, he can arrive at his ultimate goal (the glory of God). Anyone who thinks it over rationally will choose the way of the intellectual. A person who follows that way with the spirit of humility of the second mode will not only be a splendid Christian, but could even become a saint. Yet Ignatius shows the retreatant a more elevated way. It is a foolish way which only someone who has been completely captivated by Christ is able to follow 'in order to be more like Christ our Lord'. His love for Christ is so great that he wants to become as much like him as possible: 'I desire and choose poverty with Christ poor rather than riches . . . reproaches with Christ thus suffering . . . I am willing to be considered as worthless and a fool for Christ Who suffered such treatment before me.'

The super-logic of the 'fool'

The third mode of humility is a way that cannot be understood rationally. There is something in it of a higher order which the logic of reason finds incomprehensible. We might call it the logic of love or the logic of the heart. No, it is something more than that even. Perhaps we should call it a free leap in which ordinary logic does not hold good. Earlier I spoke of someone who has been completely captivated by Christ; by this I don't mean a person who loves Christ with feverish passion. I am speaking, rather, of a self-controlled, serene person who is master of his love. The real man of love is someone who is fully aware of being completely absorbed in his love and who enters *samādhi* fully awake. A person with experience in Zen would understand this immediately; he has only to reflect on the feelings of respect and affection between a Zen master and his disciple to find an analogy with it.

One more thing I would like to call attention to is the meaning of the words 'with Christ'. They do not mean that looking up to the reviled Christ as your model, you emulate him by desiring to be reviled also. That is emulating Christ, not being 'with Christ'. For me as a Christian, Christ is someone who actually exists with me. My life is sustained by the life of Christ. We all live the same life with Christ. Therefore when we live according to the impulse of this life, we live the same way Christ does and naturally want to be poor with Christ who became poor and reviled with Christ who was reviled. This is what generates the logically incomprehensible leap of life. You might say that it is the consummation of the Great Death-Great Life dynamism. It is a logic that only a 'fool' can understand, a super-logic that common sense is incapable of fathoming.

The figure of the fool Jōshū

Now, is there something in Zen analogous to this third mode of humility? Of course we will not find anything in exactly the same form and it is futile to look for similarities in wording or externals. But what about in the deepest spiritual structure? Isn't there something similar to it in the highest state of realization in Zen? In my own limited Zen practice, I have already found two instances of things that bear a resemblance to the third mode of humility. One is in the last koan of Tōzan's Five Ranks, 'Unity Attained'. In the *Hōkyō Zammai* (Jewelled-Mirror Samādhi) it is described thus: 'Travelling in disguise, he comports himself like a simpleton, like a fool.' When this point is reached, there is no longer anything called enlightenment or delusion. Already at the fourth of the Five Ranks, 'Arrival at Mutual Integration', one has passed through to the state of realization where 'The two heads [of dualism] having been cut off, a single sword hangs from heaven, cold'. Over and above that, at the Fifth Rank, you are like a stupid, runny-nosed kid meandering aimlessly down the street with a blank look on your face. Hakuin Zenji says of such a one, 'He hires some other venerable fools to bring snow and together they fill up a well with it.' Isn't there something here that also runs through the third mode of humility?

The other point of resemblance is in National Teacher Daitō's well-known comment on the koan 'Jōshū sees through an old woman'.

> All say that he carries a lamp to light his way in broad daylight. They don't know he has lost his money and is charged with the crime as well.

Let's start from the koan 'Jōshū sees through an old woman (*Mumonkan*, Case 31). A monk who was a disciple of Jōshū once asked directions from an old woman running a tea house at the foot of Mount Gotai. Apparently something of a Zen adept, the old woman replied, 'Go straight on.' When the monk had taken four or five steps, she called out in a low voice, 'He may look like a fine monk but he goes the same way as all the rest!' The monk was puzzled and later related the happening to Master Jōshū, asking him, 'What sort of person is this old woman?' Jōshū said, 'Wait! I'll go and investigate and see through that old woman for you.' The next day he went to the old woman and asked the same question that the monk had. She replied in the same way, and Jōshū walked on just like the monk. When he returned to the temple, he called all the monks together and said, 'I have completely seen through the old woman.'

Jōshū did not say what he learned or how he saw through the old woman. That is the point to be grasped in this koan. As has been said, 'Notice how he says neither right nor wrong' (Tōin Iida Rōshi). To be told, 'Go straight on', and then to be called after by the old woman, 'He may look like a fine monk, but he goes the same way as all the rest', seems to have bothered the monk. He wondered whether the old woman was only an ordinary person or whether she had an enlightened eye. Just what was her state of realization? The monk's uncertainty was a result of not having a firm grasp on his own True Self. If he had had a firm, subjective hold on it, he would have known that whether the old woman was enlightened or not, both states are a manifestation of the 'eternal life' which is the fountainhead of the True Self. And he would not have been perturbed in the least. Jōshū must have penetrated the psychological state of his disciple for he took the trouble to go out and do exactly the same thing the monk had done. At first this behaviour on Jōshū's part seems stupid. But since he did the exact same thing as the monk, we should probably call it enigmatic. Jōshū has caught the monk in the trap of an enigma and is shaking him up. And of course the old woman is using the same technique.

Comment by National Teacher Daitō: losing his money he is charged with the crime as well

This is one of the *nantō* (difficult to pass) koans. Ordinarily it is given only to a disciple who has passed the first barrier (i.e., attained enlightenment), been given a thorough cross-examination, and finished the *kikan* and *gonsen* koans. The disciple has gotten a firm grasp on his True Self through the *hosshin* koans and come to fully understand its activity through the *kikan* koans. With the *gonsen* koans he becomes capable of expressing 'the natural beauty of life' of the True Self. By giving the disciple the present koan, the master is jolting him in an effort to bring him to break through both enlightenment and delusion and attain a firm and unshakable state of realization. In order to do that, he must go back again and again to the source of the self. He must look back and reflect deeply until he can see that it is not only enlightenment, but delusion as well, that comes from this source. Then for the first time he will be able to stand on the pinnacle of the state of realization which cuts through both delusion and enlightenment. When this happens he will be able to tell the depth of another's state of realization or delusion. He will stand on the same level as Jōshū and understand what seemed to be a silly act on Jōshū's part. And, of course, the koan will solve itself.

The issue here, however, is the famous comment of National Teacher Daitō regarding 'Jōshū sees through an old woman': 'All say that he carries a lamp to light his way in broad daylight. They don't know he has lost his money and is charged with the crime as well.' When the disciple has finally passed the difficult main case of the koan, and before he has a chance to catch his breath, he is told by the master to tackle Daitō's comment. For most, this results in being raked over the coals even more. Daitō's comment means, 'All the men of old have said that Jōshū, the main character of the koan, is a simpleton who carries a lamp to light his way even though the sun is shining. But they have missed the most important thing. They don't know he has been attacked by a thief who took all his money and now is accused of being the criminal himself.' If we look into the reason why Jōshū, in spite of his great age, went out like a fool to Mount Gotai, we realize, of course, that it came from his desire to save all beings. National Teacher Daitō sees in the form of Jōshū a Bodhisattva who is not bothered by the fact that 'attacked by a thief and robbed of his money, he is accused of the crime as well.' This 'figure' of Jōshū, overflowing with kindliness, is refreshing to the eyes. There is a famous remark that has been made in regard to Daitō's comment. Hakuin Zenji, one of the greatest giants in the world of Zen, was deeply moved upon reading these words of Daitō and left us the following:

When I read this comment by National Teacher Daitō, I could not help being astonished. Without even bothering to stop to light incense, I turned in the direction of distant Kyoto and prostrated nine times. I was chagrined at my error and snapped my fingers, saying, 'Ah, National Teacher Daitō is indeed the life blood of those who follow the Buddhist Way! Not to have known such a great Zen master up to now is a great negligence on my part. The tradition that says he is the reincarnation of Unmon is no mistake. Master Setchō, compiler of the *Hekigan-roku*, is famous for his skill in interjecting comments, but National Teacher Daitō, with these words about carrying a lamp in broad daylight, far surpasses even Setchō. His comment is truly amazing and should be read carefully. It is to my shame that having only a dim eye and the shrewdness of a mere fox or badger, I have played with words and added these worthless comments.'

What a grand sight to see Daitō revering Jōshū and Hakuin Zenji, in turn, revering Daitō, as they carry on the religious tradition of Zen!

Chapter 18

Taking hold of the mystery of the cross

Great Master Ba is unwell (*Hekigan-roku*, Case 3)

The cross of Jesus (Mark 15:16-37)

The third week of the Spiritual Exercises

In this chapter I would like to consider the relation between the third week of the *Exercises* and a Zen *sesshin*. The theme of the third week is Christ's Passion. The retreatant contemplates how much Christ was made to suffer for our sins and how he willingly accepted death on the cross. Then he resolves that, just as Christ was crucified to save him, he will daily take on the sufferings of the cross with Christ. This is the gist of the third week which again, at first glance, seems to have no relation to Zen.

Working on the koan 'Great Master Ba is unwell', however, gave me a new insight into the mystery of Christ's cross. This experience made me aware of the deep connection between the third week of the *Exercises* and the practice of Zen. Therefore I would like to tell about that small experience here to show the relation between a *sesshin* and the third week of the *Spiritual Exercises*.

The koan 'Great Master Ba is unwell' was given to me after I had passed the first barrier and seven or eight additional koans. When I reflect on it now, it does not seem to be such a difficult problem, but at the time I found it very hard to pass. I went to *dokusan* some twenty times while grappling with it. This koan gave me such a struggle that it is still fresh in my mind; what I went through at the time was so impressed on me that I shall probably never forget it.

Great Master Ba was unwell. The temple superintendent asked him, 'Reverend, how is your venerable health these days?' The Great Master said, 'Sun Face Buddha, Moon Face Buddha' (*Hekigan-roku* [Blue Cliff Record] , Case 3).

Baso Dōitsu Zenji was such an excellent master that he produced eighty-four outstanding monk disciples, among them the famous Nansen and Hyakujō. He was seriously ill and near death when the worried temple superintendent came to see him and asked, 'Master, how are you?' Baso answered, 'Sun Face Buddha, Moon Face Buddha.'

Tackling the koan 'Great Master Ba is unwell'

The above is all there is to the koan 'Great Master Ba is unwell'. When it was assigned to me, I had a certain flash of intuition, which I later realized was the correct point of the koan. The moment it came to me, though, I brushed it aside as being too simple. If I had taken it and presented it to the master in *dokusan*, I might have passed the koan in one attempt. Had I done so, however, not only would I have missed the precious experience I am about to relate, but I also would not have 'realized' the koan in the true sense of the word. This has made me feel keenly that it is more important to experience each koan with the 'body' than to pass many koans.

After brushing away the flash of insight I had, I tackled the koan head-on, but could see it as nothing but a complete puzzle. I read Master Tōin Iida's *Hekigan-shū Teishōroku* (Sermons on the Blue Cliff Record) in which he said that Sun Face Buddha meant a life of one day and one night and Moon Face Buddha meant a life of 18,000 years. I still could not get the point. There was nothing to do but sit in zazen with all my might. The first solution that flashed across my mind was, 'A life of one day and night and a life of 18,000 years are exactly the same. The length of a person's life doesn't make a bit of difference.' This is a typical example of a solution that is arrived at intellectually. It is no wonder that when you take something like this into the *dokusan* room, you are driven out immediately with a ring of the

master's bell. Having intellectually apprehended the meaning
of the text, you are trying to transcend the thing indicated
(in this case, the length of life) conceptually by means of the
sense of the subject-matter. I went to *dokusan* many times
with this kind of solution, but got nowhere. I do not remember
how many times it was I had gone when the master said
just one sentence to me, 'Would a sick person on the verge
of death say something like that?'

These words hurled against my brain. I had thought I
was becoming one with the koan, but this single sentence
from the master showed me that I had just been working on
it with my head.

With this, I returned to the mind of a beginner and started
all over again. A koan expresses the Primal Face of the True
Self straightforwardly. 'That's it! I'll go back to my own self.
If I were facing death what would I do? Good! I'll push on
with this to the finish.' In this new frame of mind, I again
started to put all my strength into sitting. My whole body
was filled with energy and I began to feel that I did not care
when I died. I went to *dokusan* a number of times in this
state, but the master showed no sign of approving me. It was
as though I had been driven into a blind alley. There was no
use struggling for I could not get out if I tried. I was at a loss.
Then the master simply commented, 'I wonder if a person
like master Baso Dōitsu would say such a thing when he was
facing death.'

Getting free of the birth-death duality

That one sentence completely changed my direction. It might
be better to say that the whole of my existence suddenly
changed its course. Up to then I had been working on this
koan by applying it to myself and striving to be emancipated
from the duality of birth and death. This was worthwhile in
its own way, and I think that correspondingly I achieved
emancipation from my own birth and death. But there was a
very important blind spot in this. I may have been emancipated
from *my* birth and death, but it was not a release from
the birth-death duality itself. I did not see that Great Master

Ba's brief words were overflowing with the desire to save all beings, nor did I feel their great burning compassion. I might be unafraid at the moment of my own death, but it was questionable how I would accept the death of my parents, brothers and sisters, or friends. It was this me that my master was addressing, pressing me towards a conversion of mind. What words did the Great Master Ba utter as he was dying? I had to break loose from myself and try to become Great Master Ba. After becoming one with him, I would see what he said. Master Ba was a great teacher who produced priests of a calibre rarely seen in Zen history, such as Nansen and Hyakujō. His state of realization must have been remarkably high. I had to penetrate the very innards of this Master Ba. No, I had to become one with him. If that happened, not only would I be freed of my own birth and death, not only would I be emancipated from the birth and death of Master Ba, but directly, here and now, I would also be able to transcend the duality of birth and death itself.

I put all my energy into just sitting. The point of the koan that hit me from 'over there' was surprisingly simple. If a beginner or inexperienced person were to hear it, he would undoubtedly be astonished and think that Zen was trivial nonsense. Yet real truth is very simple. The higher the truth the simpler it becomes. In both Zen and Christianity, the person who has reached the pinnacle of truth is simple and docile, like a little child. In that simplicity, however, there lie hidden infinite riches.

For that reason, I think it is better not to write the solution of the koan here. With a view to relating my 'experience' of the cross later, however, I would like to go into some detail about how the solution came to me. When I first tried becoming one with Great Master Ba on his death bed, I felt that he was some distant entity and that his death had no relation to me. On putting forth every ounce of my energy into sitting, however, I began to perceive that Master Ba's death was not happening to a stranger but to me. Yet even then the thought was lurking in my mind that an insignificant person like me would never really be able to become one with a great man like Baso. When I became aware that this thought had been buried in my unconscious,

I cut it off and went on sitting single-mindedly.

I wonder if this is what is meant by the expression, 'To cut down the middle of the field of the eight consciousnesses with a single sword'? I disappeared; Baso disappeared; and birth and death seem to have been transcended, for the point of the koan emerged easily. There was no big struggle or fanfare. It was a simple and brief solution. At the same time there was the consciousness of being one with Great Master Ba; I knew that there was not room for a hair's breadth between us. This was not merely a spiritual realization; it was an awakening of my whole 'body'. It was not just knowing that Baso's spirit was the same as mine; his whole 'body', which was afire with the Bodhi-mind, took hold of my 'body', filling it with that same mind, until finally the 'body' of Great Master Ba gave life to my 'body' and freed it from birth and death.

The three steps in emancipation from the birth-death duality

From my personal experience with the koan 'Great Master Ba is unwell', I have found that there are three steps in the process of passing it. The first step is to reflect on the koan intellectually; the next step is to accept the koan subjectively as your own and seek to be emancipated from your own birth and death; the third step is to become one with Master Ba and directly transcend the birth-death duality itself. There is something similar to these three steps in the process of understanding the cross of Christ, which I would like to discuss next.

Shortly after passing this koan, I had an unexpected experience, one which touched the very core of Christianity. When the point of the koan emerged, it was an important experience for me, but it seems insignificant now when compared to the experience I had immediately following it. On the evening of the day that I passed the koan, I made my way home wrapped in deep peace and tranquillity. The feeling on passing a koan is indescribably exhilarating. It was particularly so for me on that day as I had solved a koan that had given me a hard struggle. Most of the priests were already asleep when I reached home; the house was wrapped in silence. As I slowly walked down the silent corridor, I had an absolutely new 'breakthrough' into the mystery of Christ's cross. It was not a devout thought that I pictured to myself intellectually. Nor was it my soul being moved by the love which Christ showed in dying on the cross. Much less was it a kind of apparition in which Christ spoke to me from the cross. To give an idea of what it was, I might call it a kind of direct intuition, a Christian awakening. Reflecting on it later, I realized that this experience was closely connected to my solving the koan 'Great Master Ba is unwell'.

The cross of Jesus

Let us first read with a silenced heart what the Bible tells us of how Jesus was crucified.

> And the soldiers led him away inside the palace (that is, the praetorium); and they called together the whole battalion. And they clothed him in a purple cloak, and plaiting a crown of thorns they put it on him. And they began to salute him, 'Hail, King of the Jews!' And they struck his head with a reed, and spat upon him, and they knelt down in homage to him. And when they had mocked him, they stripped him of the purple cloak, and put his own clothes on him. . . .
>
> And they brought him to the place called Golgotha (which means the place of a skull). And they crucified him, and divided his garments among them, casting lots for them, to decide what each should take. And it was the third hour when they crucified him. And the inscription of the charge against him read, 'The King of the Jews.' And with him they crucified two robbers, one on his right and one on his left.
>
> And those who passed by derided him, wagging their heads, and saying, 'Aha! You who would destroy the temple and build it in three days, save yourself, and come down from the cross!' So also the chief priests mocked him to one another with the scribes, saying, 'He saved others; he cannot save himself. Let the Christ, the King of Israel, come down now from the cross, that we may see and believe.' Those who were crucified with him also reviled him.
>
> And at the ninth hour Jesus cried with a loud voice, 'E'lo-i, E'lo-i, la'ma sabachtha'ni?' which means, 'My God, my God, why

hast thou forsaken me?' And some of the bystanders hearing it said, 'Behold he is calling Eli'jah'. . . . And Jesus uttered a loud cry, and breathed his last (Mark 15:16-37).

I have meditated on the cross of Jesus many hundreds of times and have daily endeavoured to carry the cross myself. Looking back, I see that twenty-eight years have passed since I first began to do so. Moreover, it has been twenty-five years since I entered the Society of Jesus. Upon entering the Society, I was taught that 'Jesuit' means a person who lives like Jesus, and this has always remained deeply impressed on me. I secretly flattered myself, therefore, that to a certain degree I knew all there was to know about the cross of Jesus. My self-conceit was thoroughly shattered by this experience, however, for it exposed how shallow and narrow in scope my understanding of the cross had been. That is why I wrote above that an absolutely new 'breakthrough' into the mystery of Christ's cross took hold of me.

The three steps in the understanding of the cross

In what way had my understanding of the cross been limited? To put it simply, it resembled the limited nature of the first and second steps in the process of passing the koan 'Great Master Ba is unwell'.

The first step in the contemplation of the cross is to recall the crucifixion of Christ, reflecting on his suffering and anguish, and suffering and being anguished with him. There are many aspects to this stage. Sometimes you may be moved to tears by feelings of sadness; at other times there are no feelings, but you resolve with your will alone to suffer with Christ for the rest of your life; or, again, your heart overflows with gratitude towards Christ who was made to endure such suffering for your sake. Such meditations on the cross are good in their own way, but as spiritual experiences they are shallow. What they all have in common is their wilful deliberation; the wilful contrivance, whether conscious or unconscious, of the person meditating is included in all the ideas, feelings and resolutions that occur in this state of mind. What is worse, the crucifixion becomes an object for meditation and is not apprehended subjectively. Much less does one think of being one with the cross of Christ.

The second step in meditating on the cross is to have, in the words of Ignatius, 'grief with Christ suffering, a broken heart with Christ heart-broken' (Exercise 207). At this stage, the primary object is to apprehend the crucifixion subjectively and participate in it oneself. The understanding of the crucifixion here is not in terms of ideas or concepts; it is an actual participation in the cross of Christ. There is a marked difference between this and the first step of the meditation. The crucifixion is not the object of meditation, but a reality which closely involves the one who is meditating. Yet the feeling that something lies between one's own cross and that of Christ still remains.

Before passing the koan 'Great Master Ba is unwell', my understanding of the crucifixion was pretty much like the above. The experience I had directly after it, though, taught me that there is not a hair's breadth between the cross of Christ and my cross. The wall between Christ and me has tumbled. This is not merely the *spirit* of Christ being one with mine; rather, the crucified Christ is one with me as I carry my own cross right now. In other words, the 'body' of the crucified Christ and my 'body' are inseparable. The 'body' of Christ on the cross, filled with the desire to save mankind, takes hold of my 'body' and fills it with that same desire, and finally my 'body' is made to live by the 'body' of Christ crucified. My 'body' lives; it is not my flesh that lives, however, but the 'body' of Christ.

To discern a structural resemblance between this 'experience' of the cross and the 'experience' of the koan 'Great Master Ba is unwell' is not so difficult. Consequently, we can see to some degree, how the third week of the *Exercises* resembles a Zen *sesshin*. What is more, this deepening of my meditation on the cross would surely never have occurred without the 'experience' of the koan 'Great Master Ba is unwell'.

Chapter 19

Examine the place where you stand

Rules to Be Observed in the Future in the Matter
of Food (Exercise 210)

Zuigan calls 'Master' (*Mumonkan*, Case 12)

Life-giving wisdom

At the end of the third week of the *Spiritual Exercises* there
is a supplement entitled 'Rules to Be Observed in the Future
in the Matter of Food'. These rules tell how a person can
discover what amount of food and drink is proper for him.
Because they appear to be related more to etiquette than to
the spiritual life, the majority of those persons who read
them undoubtedly think that Ignatius was over-particular
to make such detailed stipulations regarding temperance in
food and drink. Or at least there are probably few persons
who really understand what these rules mean. I, myself, in
spite of having read them many times, did not learn too
much from them. To me they were meaningless written rules
in a book called *The Spiritual Exercises*, but not living
rules within me.

Strangely enough, though, once I started to practise Zen,
I gradually came to see the meaning of these regulations. The
turning point, as I will relate below, came about as the result
of a living lesson by the Zen master who was directing me.
At the same time, I think that Zen practice itself was changing my state of consciousness, giving me the true wisdom to
understand these rules. As a matter of fact, they are not
something that can be apprehended intellectually; much less

can they be put into practice in everyday life merely on the basis of such an understanding. Their meaning can only be comprehended when the self has been emancipated through religious practice and the rules have already come alive in an actual situation. In such a case, even though the person concerned lacks a reflective awareness of the matters written in the rules, because he has not read them, he is already using this wisdom in his daily life. He is unaware, however, that this is wisdom.

Yet once a person who has attained this consciousness reads the rules and reflects on himself, becoming conscious of the wisdom (the 'discerning eye') that he is already using in his everyday life, he can achieve a true 'living eye'. By acquiring this 'eye' he puts new life in his daily actions and, what is most important, he is a better guide of others, especially like-minded people who are pursuing the same Way. I would like to examine the 'Rules to Be Observed in the Future in the Matter of Food' that Ignatius has left us, therefore, not only for the purpose of making a comparative study of Zen and Christianity, but also because I think that it will provide some worthwhile suggestions for those engaged in religious practice in pursuit of a true Way. As my Zen master always says, what in Buddhism is called 'right views' must be 'living right views', a kind of conscious wisdom which has been brought to the level of awareness by reflection. Wisdom which is used without this kind of awareness is still only latent wisdom, not self-conscious wisdom. The former is a *living* wisdom, but not until it becomes the latter is it a truly *vitalizing* wisdom.

Examine the place where you stand

The opportunity for my coming to know the meaning of these rules was a teaching so fundamental to the spirit of Zen that my master frequently instructed us about it. There is a famous expression in Zen 'Examine the place where you stand'. The master once explained it this way: 'At the entrance to this *dōjō* it says "Examine the place where you stand". This doesn't mean merely to straighten your shoes or wooden clogs when you take them off before entering. To put your shoes or clogs the way they should be is the work of saving all sentient beings. To examine the place where you stand means to check whatever you are doing, perceive how things should properly be, and make them so; this is the concrete putting into practice of the salvation of all beings.'

At another time during a sermon, the master said vehemently, 'Just before this talk I went into the lavatory and found that the water had been left running and the lights on. This makes me wonder why some persons are doing zazen. Water and electricity are also the life of Buddha. What's the point of passing the koan "Mu" if you can't see the Buddha-life in concrete things? Value water and use it carefully, in the way that it should be used. That's the very object of doing zazen. If you can't do this, you had better not do zazen!'

I have put the above into my own words, so it is not exactly the way the master said it. And no one could commit to writing the intensity with which he spoke. Indeed it was this very tone of voice that conveyed the master's earnest desire for the salvation of all beings. Certainly those of us who 'bodily' heard it straight from his lips will never forget it.

Now, what is the connection between these words of a Zen master and Ignatius's rules regarding meals? If we substitute food for water and electricity or for clogs and shoes, aren't they the same? To have a right view of what bread and water and fine food and liquor should be and to use them accordingly is the very thing that Ignatius is teaching with these rules. If we admit that, we can see that his detailed treatment of the subject of meals is not the fussing of an over-particular person, but the interested concern of a Bodhisattva. It is the important matter of man's salvation. Only a person like Ignatius, in possession of a true spiritual eye, could write such rules.

The question of why Ignatius placed these rules at the end of the third week has caused a great deal of controversy among many students of the *Exercises*. According to the 'General Directives', Ignatius had no special reason for putting them at the end of the third week except that there

was no other place to put them. Dissatisfied with this explanation, some persons have said that he placed them there
because the Last Supper is a topic of meditation during the
third week. Others say that the contemplation of Jesus's
Passion in the third week make it an appropriate place for
the rules since they deal with the curbing of desire. Still a
third group maintains that one must consider the period of
time in which Ignatius lived. This group says that since
most of the persons making the Exercises in those days
belonged to the intellectual and upper classes, they were
habitually eating fine food and consequently needed to be
taught moderation at table. But Ignatius did not write the
Exercises only for this type of person. In a certain respect,
all these reasons seem not to touch the core of Ignatius's
mind. In my opinion, there is a more profound reason for
these rules being placed at the end of the third week.

Ignatius thought of the formal Exercises as a one-month
religious practice. Furthermore, he felt that in order to
make them, a person must be of firm purpose and outstanding disposition. Such a person, as I mentioned above, has
gone through a thorough purification in the first week of the
Exercises and in the second week has responded whole-
heartedly to Christ's call, resolving to make a 'more precious
and important gift'. In the third week, burning with the
resolve to suffer with the suffering Christ and to be broken-
hearted with the heartbroken Christ, he should have already
advanced to a fairly high state of realization. There is no
doubt that it is to this kind of retreatant that Ignatius is
giving the rules regarding food. Now, would he be preaching
moderation to such a person? If so, he lacked the eye to
discern others. Yet as far as one can judge from the
Monumento Ignatiana (the memoirs compiled by his disciples
after his death), there have been few persons in the Christian
world who could see as well as Ignatius into a disciple's
personality, disposition, and state of realization and direct
him appropriately.

Meals are the scene of life and death

What sort of guiding principles would a good director give a retreatant in such a lofty state of consciousness? In another week, having completed the month-long Exercises, the retreatant will be returning to his everyday life. How should he put what he has learned in the Exercises into actual practice day by day? The problem he will come up against is how to relate to the world, and one of the most concrete places that this happens is at table. Not only are meals the first situation that one encounters in terms of practically applying the wisdom learned from the Exercises, but they also hold the central place in man's relationship with the world. When a person takes food into his body, to make the food come alive or to kill it and, by means of this process, to keep alive or kill his own body, depends on the common actions called eating and drinking. Not only are they the junction between subject and object, but they are also the point where harmony may diverge into discord. Indeed, it would be closer to the reality to call these acts the scene of life and death, the front line of the battle. To have a 'discerning eye' regarding meals is to hold the key to the victory. If a person has this 'eye', he not only controls his meals and vitalizes both the food and his own body, but his potential for relating successfully in other situations is also increased. In this sense, having an 'eye' in matters of food and drink will surely play a pivotal role in the retreatant's daily life.

In addition, as I mentioned before, these rules regarding meals cannot be understood intellectually; only a person who has already been emancipated and is living them in an actual situation can really grasp them. Isn't the retreatant who has completed the Exercises through the third week, therefore, the most suitable person to read them? We can even say that the only persons capable of reading and comprehending them are those who have done this kind of religious practice. To reflect on the rules in this fashion solves, I think, the problem of why Ignatius put them at the end of the third week of the Exercises.

Ignatius divides the rules into eight parts. Limitations of space prohibit an explanation of them all, but let me mention in detail some points of special interest. In particular, I would like to focus on our central subject, a 'discerning eye'.

The first, second and third rules teach abstinence (*la abstinencia*) in regard to bread, wine and supplementary foods. Abstinence ordinarily means abstaining from food or fasting, but the context indicates that this is not the meaning here. I think, instead, that in this case it means discretion or self-control, the ability to refrain or not refrain from eating these foods. The first rule pertains to bread, but since there is less chance of the appetite being uncontrolled (*desordenar*) in regard to bread than to other foods, it says that abstinence is not so necessary. The second rule deals with wine and says that 'abstinence is more appropriate (*más cómmoda*)' in this case than with regard to eating bread. Ignatius was aware that the degree of abstinence necessary varied with the person; that is why he said, 'Therefore (*por lo tanto*) one must consider carefully (*mucho mirar*) what would be beneficial to him and therefore permissible, and also what would be harmful, and so to be avoided' (Exercise 211).

Abstinence and a 'discerning eye'

As we know from personal experience, it is very difficult to be self-controlled in regard to alcoholic drinks. Ignatius is not preaching the giving-up of alcohol as the stoics or moralists do; the issue is, rather, the proper amount of alcohol to be consumed. Or, to put it more precisely, the question is how much a person judges to be the proper amount for him or herself. Ignatius expressly says, 'One must carefully consider . . .'. The word translated in English as *consider* is the Spanish *mirar*. It means to turn one's gaze upon and look well, observe closely, direct one's attention to, think over well, and so forth. I think what Ignatius wanted to express with this word was the 'discerning eye' to look carefully and recognize the proper amount of alcohol for onself. We should notice, moreover, the relation between a 'discerning eye' and abstinence. If one has the ability to stop drinking or to drink if he pleases, i.e. 'abstinence', it is not so difficult to have this 'eye'. In the case of alcoholic liquors, not only is more 'abstinence' (self-control) necessary, but it is also very important to make good use of one's 'discerning eye'. If not, the appetite tends to be 'uncontrolled (*desordenar*)'. The antonym of *ordenar* (order), *desordenar* means to fail to maintain the proper harmony between things. To use the words of the Zen master quoted above, *desordenar* is not to use alcohol as it should be used, and *ordenar* is to use it as it should be used.

The rule of most interest is the fourth. It says that 'while taking care not to become sick, the more a person abstains in the quantity of food suited or agreeable (*lo conviniente*) to him, the sooner he will arrive (*alcanzará*) at the mean (*el medio*) he should observe in eating and drinking' (Exercise 213). As is often said, we who live in an age of material abundance generally overeat. It was the same in the time of Ignatius. An amount that is *lo conviniente* refers to the food in which we overindulge without being conscious of it. Ignatius is urging the retreatant to become aware of his own overeating. He urges him not to eat until he has become comfortably satisfied and says that he should control himself by gradually correcting his concealed *desordenar* and giving food and drink their proper form. He states that the more a person decreases the 'suitable amount' the sooner he will arrive at the mean (the true suitable amount) for himself. The words *will arrive at* are important. The original *alcanzar* means to attain to, come up with, arrive at, finally obtain, comprehend, catch sight of, hear, and so forth. The use of the future tense is also very significant. This is in contrast to the stipulation in the second rule regarding wine which says, 'One must consider carefully what would be beneficial to him . . . and also what would be harmful.' In the second rule the retreatant is called upon to exert himself actively, but in the fourth it says that the more one decreases the agreeable amount (*lo conviniente*), in other words, to the degree that a person has the mental attitude of abstinence, he will comprehend it naturally. I think this is the reason why Ignatius used the word *alcanzar* and why he put it in the future tense; it is also why abstinence and a 'discerning eye' are so closely related. It seems to me that this is precisely the same thing as the 'right views' to which so much importance is attached in Zen. A true 'discerning eye' originates by itself out of the state of Mu which transcends the dualism of whether or not to drink alcoholic beverages. This is also the meaning underlying the teaching by my Zen master which I related above.

The actualization of 'right views'

The 'right views' of Zen and the words of Ignatius 'arriving at the mean' are similar in an even more important respect. The resemblance can be detected in the two reasons that Ignatius gives for saying 'the sooner he will arrive':

> First, by thus helping and disposing himself he will more frequently feel (*sentriá*) the interior directions, consolations, and divine inspirations that will show him the mean that is proper for him (*para mostrarsele*). Second, if he find that with such abstinence he lacks sufficient health and strength for the Spiritual Exercises, he will easily be able to judge (*fácilmente vendrá a juzgar*) what is more suitable for sustaining his body.

In these sentences Ignatius depicts the actualization of arriving at the mean 'from above' and 'from below'. First, by means of illumination from above 'the mean will reveal itself and become visible [*mostrarsele* has this meaning]'. Here it also states that it is not a matter of trying to see, but of coming to see naturally. Of course, it is presupposed that one has been prepared for this through abstinence. In Zen terms, it is to die the Great Death and actualize the Great Life. If there is a Great Death then there is a Great Life and 'right views' are born of its radiance.

Neither does Ignatius ignore the illumination 'from below'. He takes up the concrete (discriminative) aspect of losing the physical strength and energy to make the Exercises. It is by looking at this concrete aspect that one becomes able to judge a 'suitable amount'. Here, too, he says it is not a matter of making an effort, but that one will become able to judge naturally. Ignatius thus considers the problem from both the higher and lower aspects, but he is speaking about two phases of a single occurrence. He is referring to the actualization of arriving at the mean, saying that in both phases one will understand the mean, the suitable amount, naturally. Such comprehension is not acquired intellectually, but comes out of the Great Death and Great Life. Or, we might say that the actualization of arriving at the mean is one aspect of the Great Life.

If we were to put it in Zen terms, the aspect 'from above' would probably correspond to the first of Tōzan's Five Ranks, 'The Apparent within the Real', and the aspect 'from below' to the second, 'The Real within the Apparent'. Both are essentially one event, which is the third rank, 'The Coming from within the Real'.

Let me explain this in a little more detail. 'The Apparent within the Real' is the level where one sees all phenomena from the standpoint of penetration into the Absolute Nothingness of one's Primal Face or True Self. In the rules of Ignatius given above, the aspect 'from above' is to come in touch with the Divine Source, which transcends all limitations, and view material food in that light. If we admit this, there would seem to be a mutual correspondence between the two. 'The Real within the Apparent' is the level where one sees all concrete things and events in this world as equal in themselves. Then in the rules of Ignatius, the aspect 'from below' is to discern the 'true suitable amount' of food from the concrete aspect of whether one can actually maintain bodily strength and energy while decreasing the amount of food eaten. A structural similarity is apparent between these two things. Furthermore, the *real* of 'The Coming from within the Real' means that all concrete matters, as they are in themselves, are the True Self and their emergence is 'The Coming from within the Real'. In the Ignatian rules, both aspects, 'from above' and 'from below', are one from the beginning and it is from here that judgment of the 'true suitable amount' comes forth of its own accord. This is structurally similar to 'The Coming from within the Real' of the Five Ranks of Zen. I do not mean that what Ignatius is saying in the fourth rule is exactly the same as this 'Coming from within the Real', but it seems to me that we can say that they are similar in terms of intrinsic structure. I would like to present this point to my readers for their further consideration.

Master of himself (señor de sí)

Another interesting point is in the seventh rule where Ignatius teaches that losing self, one 'must take care that his mind is not entirely occupied in what he is eating, and that he is not carried away by his appetite into eating hurriedly' (Exercise 217). He also says that it is important for a person to be master of himself (*señor de sí*) both in the way that he eats and the amount that he eats. The expression 'master of himself' reminds me of a case in the *Mumonkan*, 'Zuigan calls "master" ':

> Every day Master Zuigan Shigen would call, 'Master!' to himself and answer, 'Yes?' Again he would call, 'Thoroughly awake, thoroughly awake!' and answer, 'Yes! Yes!' 'Don't be deceived by others any time or day.' 'No! No!' (*Mumonkan*, Case 12)

Zuigan Zenji, who lived in the ninth century, was a disciple of the famous Master Gantō. It is said that every day he would practice Zen by calling to himself, 'Master!' and answering, 'Yes!' 'Be wide awake,' he would say. 'Yes!' 'Don't be fooled later by anyone!' 'No, I won't!' was his spirited reply.

What is at issue here is not the admonishing of oneself to live an ethical life. Therefore 'Master' does not refer to a subject who performs moral acts; much less is it an ego that is a slave to its environment. The 'Master' in this koan is 'Your Primal Face before your parents were born'. To put it more simply, it is the Buddha-life. The problem presented by the koan is to be personally vitalized by the life of Buddha and become your own Master. Merely to be free of domination by the environmental world is insufficient. Nor is it enough to use the world as you please. To be a true 'Master' is to be aware that the environmental world is also the Buddha-life and to make it come alive and realize its full potential.

Zuigan, the main character of this koan, was not just mechanically calling 'Master!' and answering 'Yes!' He had become a 'Master', in the true sense of the word, in everything, whether it was properly arranging his footgear on entering the house, using water carefully, or taking a proper amount of food at meals. This is what Rinzai means when he says, 'If you are Master everywhere, the Truth is everywhere you are.' Now, is what Ignatius says in his 'Rules to Be Observed in the Future in the Matter of Food' so different, I wonder, from what has been said about 'Zuigan calls "Master" '?

Chapter 20

The cross is the resurrection

Nansen kills a cat (*Mumonkan*, Case 14)

The cross and resurrection of Jesus

The fourth week of the Exercises

In this final chapter, I would like to investigate the resemblance between the fourth week of the *Exercises* and a Zen *sesshin*. The theme of the fourth week is Christ's resurrection. According to the New Testament account, three days after Christ died on the cross, he rose from the dead and appeared often to his disciples. The retreatant meditates on this historical event and participates in 'the great glory and joy of Christ'. As I have repeatedly mentioned, by the third week of the *Exercises*, the retreatant has realized that he and Christ live by the same divine life, so that to participate joyfully in the glory of Christ's resurrection is nothing but the realization that the retreatant himself is also animated by the same life of the resurrection. Not until a Christian rises to this level of awareness will he be able to live, like Christ, just as the vital force of the resurrection impels him, freely and creatively spending his own life for others. This is a synopsis of the fourth week, which at first may seem to have nothing to do with a Zen *sesshin*.

Strangely enough, though, my study of Zen, even though it has no connection with the resurrection, gave me a deeper understanding of it. It is my hope that by relating this experience I will give the reader a deeper insight into what similarities there are between the fourth week of the *Spiritual Exercises* and a *sesshin*.

I have learned two things from Zen that have helped me understand the cross and resurrection. One is that the killing sword is, at the same time, the life-giving sword. The second is the meaning of Dōgen Zenji's statement, 'The whole universe is man's real body'. These two things have shed great light on my deeper realization of Christ's resurrection. Let me try to relate the first of these experiences.

It was when I was working on the famous koan, 'Nansen kills a cat'. I had already looked at a number of other koans and learned through them the Zen spirit of dying the Great Death; I had also grasped, to some extent, the 'killing sword'. In addition, I had experienced the actualization of the Great Life with my own body and realized in part the meaning of the 'life-giving sword'. At the level I was on before working on 'Nansen kills a cat', however, I was lacking something very important. Of course, at the time this deficiency was not apparent to me.

The 'awful figure' of Nansen

In Hakuin's systemization of the koans, 'Nansen kills a cat' belongs to the *kikan* (interlockings of differentiation) koans. A practitioner working on the *kikan* koans should already have passed several *hosshin* koans and thoroughly penetrated his 'Primal Face before his parents were born'. Nevertheless, with that alone he is apt to remain in the world of equality of absolute Mu and his realization degenerate into a false equality. By pondering the *kikan* koans, therefore, he is made to step back into the everyday world of discrimination and achieve freedom of activity. Through this the Zen practitioner masters living resourcefulness in all circumstances and learns the vigorous functioning of the whole. What sort of vigorous functioning of the whole, then, is one supposed to acquire with 'Nansen kills a cat'?

> The monks of the eastern and western Zen halls were quarrelling about a cat. Nansen held it up and said, 'Monks, if one of you can say a word, I'll spare the cat. If you can't, I'll put it to the sword.'

No one could respond so Nansen finally slew it. When Jōshū came back in the evening, Nansen told him what had happened. Jōshū took off his straw sandals, put them on top of his head and left. Nansen said, 'If you had been there I could have spared the cat' (*Mumonkan*, Case 14).

In the *dokusan* room, this koan is looked at in two parts. The first part concludes with 'So Nansen finally slew it'. The numerous monks in Nansen's monastery were divided between the eastern and western halls. One day the monks of the two halls were having an argument about a cat. Men are the same everywhere in the world: they will never cease to quarrel as long as they view things dualistically. In that sense, this koan is a living problem for us even now. It has an important role to play in cutting off our dualistic views in the concrete situations of everyday life.

Hearing this quarrel going on, Nansen must have seen it as a golden opportunity. With the speed of lightning, he grabbed the cat by the neck and shoved it before the eyes of the monks, challenging them, 'See if you can say a living word. If you can, I'll spare this cat. If not, I'll kill it with one stroke of my sword. Well? Speak up! Say something!' Not a monk could respond; a heavy silence reigned. Finally Nansen cut the cat in two with his sword.

What overwhelmed me most when I was working on this koan was the awful 'figure' of Nansen, not because I felt it cruel to kill a cat or that he was awful because of his brutality. I was astonished, rather, by his Zen activity which spared *nothing*, not just the cat: 'If you meet the Buddha kill him, if you meet a Patriarch kill him.' Furthermore, it was a vibrant and desperate plea to the quarrelling men of the eastern and western halls. They could not be saved until they cut off all dualistic concepts, and so this killing of the cat by Nansen was a terrible living expression of his desire to save mankind.

A good deal of hard religious practice was necessary, however, for this awful 'figure' of Nansen to overwhelm my heart. As Mumon says, 'To attain marvellous enlightenment, you must completely cut off all the delusive thoughts of the ordinary mind.' It is not a simple matter to understand the True Face of Nansen.

That is because, as Engo tells us in his introductory words to 'Nansen kills a cat' in the *Hekigan-roku* (Case 63), Nansen's state of realization is in a place that 'cannot be reached by thought' and 'is unattainable through words'. Determined to die the Great Death, I confronted this 'figure' of Nansen which is unreachable by thought. Perhaps what happened then is what is meant by the expression 'to die the Great Death and be born again'. The 'awful figure' of Nansen took hold of my completely stilled mind. At the same time, for the one who 'cannot be reached by thought' (Nansen and myself), there was no distinction between the cat and self, and I understood that even the monks who were standing there with blank looks on their faces, unable to respond, were not unrelated to me. Nansen did not only kill the cat. He killed himself and the monks as well, with a single stroke of his sword. The moment I saw that, the answer to the koan came forth very simply. Uniting with Nansen, I became the cat completely and realized bodily that I too had been killed, so that when I bodily demonstrated what I had experienced, it was naturally the proper solution to the koan.

The 'awfulness' of God the Father

For some reason, after passing the first half of this koan, I received a fresh illumination in regard to the mystery of the crucifixion. I wrote earlier, when discussing the similarities between the third week of the *Exercises* and a *sesshin*, that I had already made a new 'breakthrough' into this mystery after solving the koan 'Great Master Ba is unwell'. This was unquestionably a powerful experience for me.

The crucifixion is an infinite mystery, however, and it is clear that my tiny experience could never exhaust it. What I had come to understand should rather be called ignorance when compared to this infinite mystery. That is why I have to say that what 'Great Master Ba is unwell' taught me was nothing more than a small part of the reality of the cross. It is not surprising, therefore, that 'Nansen kills a cat' should have thrown new light on it. I hope that by continuing to work on koans I will be able to draw even nearer to this infinite mystery in the future.

The new illumination that 'Nansen kills a cat' gave to my understanding of the crucifixion concerned the relation of God the Father to the cross. The insight I got from 'Great Master Ba is unwell' was the realization that I, as I carry my own cross right now, am one with Christ crucified. Working on 'Nansen kills a cat' showed me the 'awful figure' of the Father who nailed His beloved and only Son Jesus to the cross.

Christian teaching tells us that man alienated himself from God, his true Source, by original sin and built a wall between himself and God which was insurmountable from the side of man. This wall is the source of all dualistic separation. The ultimate cause of all discord such as the opposition of body and mind, the struggle between reason and passion, breaches between men, fights between races, and wars between nations, lies in this severing of relations between God and man. There is only one way out of this predicament: it is to break down the wall between God and man and become one. In Zen terminology, it is the same as saying that God is man and man is God. This was the very reason for Christ's incarnation. Being God, Christ is also man, and at the same time that he is man, he is also God. In him, the words 'God is man and man is God' are actualized in perfect form. We can say, therefore, that the salvation of mankind has been accomplished in principle in Christ.

Wanting this reality to blossom and bear fruit, the Father desired that His beloved Son die on the cross and expiate the sins of mankind. The more we reflect on this earnest desire of God the Father for the salvation of all men, the more we must call it 'awful'. What a tragic mystery — this compassionate desire that would cause Him to kill even His own beloved Son. Yet I think I could understand in part this 'awful love' of the Father when I pondered the koan 'Nansen kills a cat'. As he watched the monks of the eastern and western halls arguing over the cat, Nansen must have intuited the depth of the root of man's delusive passions. It was clear that there could be no salvation unless this root of dualistic opposition was cut off with a single stroke. This is what produced the dreadfulness of Nansen's action: 'If you meet the Buddha, kill him, if you meet a Patriarch, kill him.' Nansen only killed a cat, but God the Father slew His beloved Son. Moreover, He did it by putting him to death on the cross. Has there ever been a more appalling and sublime event in the history of the world? Yet we should not overlook the radiance of God the Father's awful compassion in this tragic event.

Before I began to practise Zen, I had some understanding of this compassionate desire of the Father; it was even my favourite subject for meditation. But that appreciation was a being overwhelmed by God the Father's love and was mainly emotional. Besides, it was still an enigma to me why the God of Love would do such a cruel thing. Clearly, in order to solve this mystery, one 'must completely cut off all the delusive thoughts of the ordinary mind'. This awful compassion of God the Father is a mystery that 'cannot be reached by thought' and 'is unattainable through words'. To become emotional and weep over God's love will never solve it. It can be understood for the first time when you extinguish all emotions and ordinary human thoughts and, without any distinction between yourself and Christ, become one with the Father. Through zazen, I came closer to this place which 'cannot be reached by thought'. Once as I was doing so, the 'awful figure' of the Father filled my completely stilled mind. I understood that by killing His Son, the Father, who knew the deep-rootedness of man's sin, had effectively smashed the wall between God and man. The Father killed not only His Son but all men as well and raised them again to a new life. He killed sinful man and created a new man who lives by the divine life.

The splendid rapport between master and disciple

Leaving the first part of the koan 'Nansen kills a cat', let us investigate the second half. On the day that Nansen killed the cat, his disciple Jōshū was out and did not return to the monastery until evening. When he came back, Nansen told him what had happened that day and asked him, 'If you had been here, what would you have done?' Jōshū silently took off his straw sandals, put them on top of his head, and left the room. At first glance this behaviour of Jōshū seems very odd. He took the things he had been wearing on his feet and put them on his head. His act appears so bizarre because we think that feet and footwear are dirty or base and that heads and headwear are somehow of more value. For the person who thinks that a cat is a lower animal and man the lord of creation, this act of Jōshū's is the height of incomprehensibility. But what if you were to transcend the dualistic relativism of feet and heads, sandals and hats, cats and humans, and see everything as a symbol of the Buddha-life? Jōshū, like his teacher Nansen, had transcended all dualism and arrived at the place that 'cannot be reached by thought'. Going beyond the distinction between self and cat and the opposition of clean and dirty, he was looking at everything from the standpoint of eternal life. That must be why he understood that it was exceedingly appropriate to have sandals on top of his head and that the life of the cat was the same as his life.

I passed the second part of the koan with comparative ease. Then, as a cross-examining question, the master gave me Inzan's comment on it, 'This old robber!' This gave me a difficult time, but breaking through it taught me the meaning of complete negation in Zen. Then, at the final *dokusan* on this koan, the master taught me, in regard to the koan as a whole, that while the first half is the killing sword and the second half the life-giving sword, the killing sword is precisely the life-giving sword. I did not grasp what he was saying immediately, but had a premonition that there was something profound there. Led by this premonition, I meditated on the master's words and came to appreciate to some extent the exquisite beauty of the Zen experience: that the killing sword and life-giving sword are dynamically one.

The important question, however, is what it is that binds the killing and life-giving swords together with the word 'is' in the phrase 'the killing sword is the life-giving sword'. This is not logical identity or a creation of rational thought. Rather, what brings this 'is' into being is the dynamic conversion of the whole person. It is nothing other than the person who has died the Great Death and come to life again. To adapt it more concretely to this particular koan, we can say that it is the person of Nansen and Jōshū.

The favourite disciple Jōshū, completely entering into Nansen's mind, expressed the last half of 'the killing sword is the life-giving sword' by putting his sandals on top of his head. In killing the cat, Nansen presented the first half, the killing sword, but by this act he was already expressing the second half, the life-giving sword. The blind disciples were incapable of seeing this, but not Jōshū. 'Jōshū took off his straw sandals, put them on top of his head, and left.' By this strange action he pushed to the fore the life-giving sword Master Nansen had been silently expressing and manifested it. With this, the spiritual reality of 'the killing sword is the life-giving sword' was completed. It is astonishing to see the rapport between Master Nansen and his favourite disciple Jōshū as they splendidly extol this spiritual reality.

Before pondering the koan 'Nansen kills a cat', I had understood the killing sword and the life-giving sword as two separate things. Passing the koan made me realize that they are dynamically identical. As a consequence, I had a new insight into Christ's resurrection.

The cross is the resurrection

The resurrection of Christ is inseparably related to his death on the cross. This is best shown by the prayer that he made to the Father just before he was crucified: 'Father, the hour has come; glorify Thy Son that the Son may glorify Thee' (John 17:1). We can understand from this that Christ is confirming that at the same time the glory of the Father is revealed by the crucifixion, the Father means also to show forth the glory of His Son Christ. This is also expressed in the following words of Jesus, 'The hour has come for the Son of Man to be glorified. Truly, truly, I say to you, unless a grain of wheat falls into the earth and dies, it remains alone; but if it dies, it bears much fruit' (John 12:23-24).

In the eyes of Christ, death on the cross is directly linked with glory. When viewed with a spiritual eye, there is no question but that death and resurrection should be directly linked by 'is', just as in the case of the Great Death and Great Life. If Christ had not been clearly aware of this, he would not have said before being crucified, 'The hour has come for the Son of Man to be glorified.' The cross is the resurrection; the resurrection is the cross. What directly connects these two with 'is' is neither the logic of theology nor an illusion created by emotional conjecture. What brings 'is' into being is the saving act of the Father and the Son. That 'is' of 'the cross is the resurrection' is the God-man Christ himself who died on the cross and rose again.

There can be no doubt that the beloved Son entered completely into the mind of the Father and became one with Him to carry out the work of man's salvation. As I said before, the Father showed such 'awful love' that he desired death on the cross for his only beloved Son. Submitting himself to this 'awful love' and becoming one with the Father, Christ revealed the terrible mystery that the cross *is* the resurrection. Just as Nansen and Jōshū united in magnificently extolling the dynamic spirit of 'the killing sword *is* the life-giving sword', here God the Father and Christ the Son become one and actualize the spiritual reality that 'the cross *is* the resurrection'.

Since we are not awake to this spiritual reality, we think death on the cross is cruel and hateful and the resurrection, on the contrary, joyous and desirable. That is why the cross and resurrection are not seen as directly connected. It is this dualistic outlook that Zen despises. As long as a person retains such a viewpoint, he will remain in complete ignorance of the mystery that the cross *is* the resurrection. If he transcends the dualistic opposites of life and death and the cross and the resurrection, however, and attains the realization that everything is a manifestation of the divine life, he will be able to realize a completely new reality.

Dōgen Zenji declares that 'Life-and-death itself is the life of Buddha.' In the same manner, can we not say that the cross-and-resurrection itself is the life of God? The divine life throbs in both the crucifixion and the resurrection, and the two are directly linked by 'is'.

But to realize that the cross is the resurrection, we too

must carry the cross with Christ. We will not bodily experience this reality until we submit ourselves with Christ to the throbbing of the divine life. There is no other way to do it.

If we can realize the truth that the cross is the resurrection, we will be able to live as the divine life impels us, freely and creatively spending our lives for mankind. Suffering and death are also the life of God; it is self-evident, then, that suffering, death and all the adversities of life are, at the same time, the resurrection (rebirth in the divine life). What a wonderful life is in store for the person who awakens to this fact and becomes one with the pulsating of the divine life!